LITTLE BOOK OF

SUPER HEROES

Mike Gent and **Michael Heatley**

LITTLE BOOK OF

SUPER HEROES

First published in the UK in 2009

www.G2ent.co.uk

Printed and bound in China

ISBN 978-1-907803-27-7

Contents

The History of the Superhero

▶ Heroic Tarzan in a rescue to save a drowning female.

Superheroes – fictional characters fighting evil with superhuman powers, gadgets and way-out weapons – have fascinated us ever since Superman first donned his cape and tights back in 1938. This is their story.

If a superhero can be defined as a benevolent being with extraordinary abilities, then its origins can be traced back to ancient myths and legends, particularly those of Hercules from the Greek and Roman eras. Edwardian fiction gave the world its first hero with a secret identity in the Scarlet Pimpernel, while Edgar Rice Burroughs' characters Tarzan and John Carter of Mars were further prototypes. Philip Wylie's 1930 novel *Gladiator* influenced the creation of Superman in that its protagonist was a biologically enhanced superhuman. Pulp magazines of the Thirties were the forerunners of comic books where Doc Savage, trained to near-superhuman status, and masked vigilantes the Spider and the Shadow anticipated the superhero.

Lee Falk's newspaper strip character the Phantom had the distinction of being the first masked comic character. The rather more obscure the Clock was the first masked hero created specifically for comic books, but it was the coming of Superman in 1938 which marked

the true start of the genre. All the defining elements – superhuman abilities, colourful costume and secret identity – were in place for the first time and it's no coincidence that the genre took its name from him.

American comics had their origins in promotional giveaways reprinting newspaper strips in the mid-Thirties. Sold separately, the comics still relied on reprints. DC was amongst the first to feature original material, generally a mix of funnies, Westerns, detective stories and other fiction genres.

It took a year for Superman to attract the attention of other publishers and to generate imitations; DC were quick to sue to protect their main asset. The superhero began to acquire more weird and wonderful powers and, by 1940, was dominating the comic book. DC also published Batman, initially at least, a darker variation on the theme, and the first successfulsuperheroine, Wonder Woman.

Pitting superheroes against supervillains seems obvious, in retrospect, but the idea took a while to evolve. In his early adventures Superman was a champion of the oppressed taking on crooked cops, corrupt politicians and shady businessmen before increasingly fantastic foes began to appear. The first supervillain appeared a year after his debut, in the shape of the Ultra-Humanite, a mad, wheelchair-bound scientist who could transplant his brain into other bodies. By 1940, the supervillain was gaining ground with another mad scientist, Lex Luthor, encountering Superman for the first time. Around the same time, Batman had his first run-in with the Joker, the most imaginative and chilling supervillain to date.

The period from the first appearance of Superman until the end of the Second World War is known as the Golden Age of Comics and represents the heyday of the superhero. Sales of a million copies were not uncommon for the most popular titles and American newsstands bulged with the cheaply-produced, colourful publications. The United States' entry into the war had been pre-empted by Timely's Captain America which featured Hitler and the Nazis as villains. Comics became part of the county's war effort as superheroes took on the Axis powers, and their patriotic exploits were eagerly devoured by many GIs.

The superhero became indelibly identified in the mind of the American public with the war. So much so in fact, that peace brought a sharp decline in its popularity – by 1947, the genre was old news. By the early Fifties, the vast majority of superhero titles had been replaced by Westerns, crime, true romance and horror. The comic-book industry was decimated in the middle of the decade when psychiatrist Dr Fredric Wertham denounced comics in *Seduction Of The Innocent*, aimed mainly at horror and crime comics but notoriously inferring a homosexual relationship between Batman and Robin.

When a Senate Investigation, complete with televised hearings, examined the medium's alleged corrupting influence on the young, publishers responded by banding together to create a self-regulatory

◀ *Action Comics* No. 1 featuring the first appearance of Superman.

▶ Superman, Batman and Robin selling US War Bonds to sink the 'Japanazis' in the Second World War.

▼ More war heroics in *Marvel Comics*.

system in 1954. The simplistic 'good must always triumph over evil' precepts of the *Comics Code* inadvertently helped pave the way for the return of the superhero.

Since the horror-comics scandal, the comic-book field had shrunk drastically with many publishers going out of business. Superman, Batman and Wonder Woman were the only superheroes that had remained in continuous publication since the war. In September 1957, editor Julius Schwartz reached back into the Golden Age hero to resurrect the Flash in a new incarnation, ushering in the Silver Age of Comics. This success was followed by new versions of other DC characters and, in 1960, Schwartz revived the idea of a team of heroes pioneered in Justice Society of America. The Justice League of America was born.

The healthy sales the title enjoyed prompted rival publisher Martin Goodman to follow suit. His company, formerly known as Timely and Atlas, had almost closed after a distribution crisis in 1957. Rather than imitating DC or reviving the company's Golden Age heroes, Stan Lee and artist Jack Kirby created the Fantastic Four. In contrast to DC's straightforward, plot-driven approach where Justice League members were virtually interchangeable, Marvel's heroes had human problems and weaknesses, even disabilities. Their adventures were set in real-world locations like New York, not fictional cities like Gotham or Metropolis.

Reviving an old trademark, the company became Marvel Comics and a remarkable burst of creativity from 1961 to 1964 saw the Incredible Hulk, Spider-Man, Thor, Avengers, X-Men, Iron Man and Daredevil hit the newsstands in quick succession. These enduring characters laid the foundations for Marvel's growth and ensured they matured into DC's major competitor in the superhero field. By the mid-Sixties comics were again dominated by the superhero and the two had become synonymous in

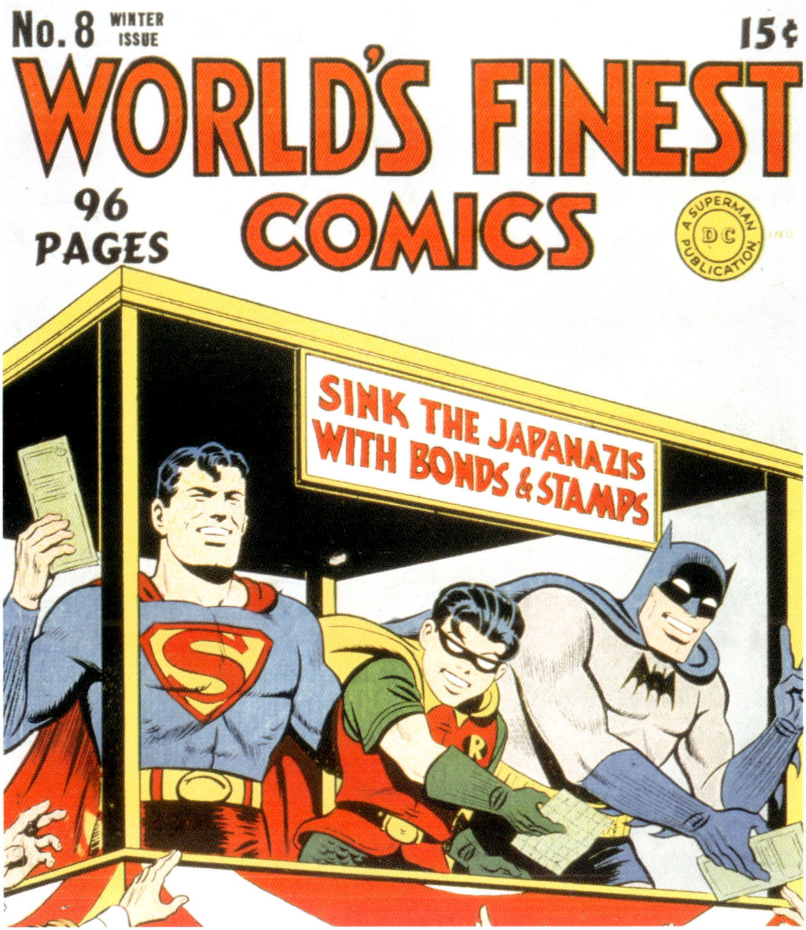
No. 8 WINTER ISSUE
15¢
WORLD'S FINEST COMICS
96 PAGES
A SUPERMAN DC PUBLICATION
SINK THE JAPANAZIS WITH BONDS & STAMPS
R

▶ Superheroes came in all shapes and sizes.

▶▶ *Spider-Man Comics Weekly*.

the eyes of the American public.

Marvel's approach was very different to that of DC. Its heroes often had feet of clay and were bedevilled by money worries and problems in their love lives. *The Amazing Spider-Man,* a combination of superheroics and soap opera, became the publisher's flagship title. Marvel's other great asset was Jack Kirby whose dynamic art became the house style. Together with Lee, he set the template for successive superheroes creators to follow.

Towards the end of the Sixties, Marvel was freed from the restrictive terms of the agreement with its distributor, a company owned by DC, allowing it to expand and eventually overtake DC in the marketplace. Although there were occasional spikes, such as the one inspired by the *Batman* television series, comic-book sales were in decline and this situation was to continue through the Seventies. Comics were selling to the hardcore superhero fan rather than the general public.

Fashions began to change in the early Seventies with a tendency towards increased realism and social consciousness; the issue of drugs was tackled in two issues of Spider-Man and in DC's *Green Lantern/Green Arrow.* As the decade drew to a close, the antihero was gaining popularity, with Batman returning to his roots as a vigilante and the new X-Men's Wolverine becoming one of Marvel's leading characters. The Seventies also saw the creation of the Punisher, a vengeance-obsessed killer; this would turn out to be a sleeper hit whose time came in the Nineties. The darker trend continued into the Eighties with Frank Miller's reworking of Daredevil.

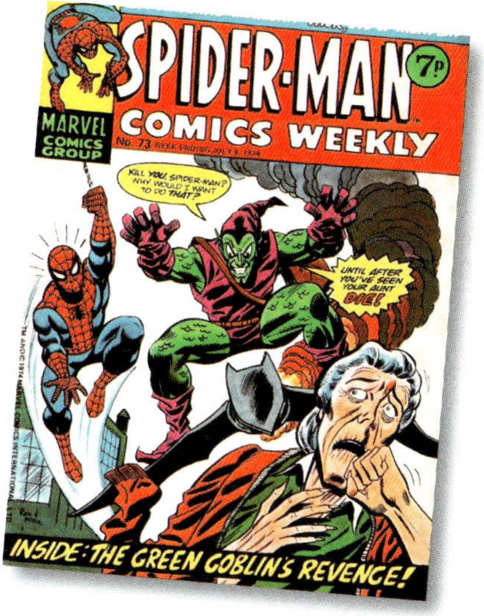

▶ Spider-Man, the hero from *Marvel Comics*.

The first challenge to the domination of Marvel and DC arrived in the early Eighties when independent publishers like Pacific and Eclipse pioneered the direct-sales market. Their comics were sold only in specialist shops on a non-returnable basis, rather than the traditional sale or return practice enjoyed by the newsstands. This was hailed as both the saviour of the comics industry and the final nail in its coffin as a mass medium. Direct sales allowed publishers greater freedom to experiment with formats like limited series, as they were no longer tied to the traditional open-ended runs of titles. Most of the material was still broadly within the superhero field.

Deconstruction became the buzzword for the mid-Eighties. The concept was highlighted in two of the most celebrated superhero series of all, neither of which would have been possible before direct sales. The British pairing of writer Alan Moore and artist Dave Gibbons examined the effects of superheroes in the real world in *Watchmen* for DC whilst, for the same company, Frank Miller's

▶ From the Silver Age of Comics.

▶▶ *Marvel Comics*' Human Torch.

The Dark Knight Returns provided a visceral tale of an alternate-future Batman.

DC simplified its convoluted parallel-world continuity in their pioneering 1985 'event' series *Crisis On Infinite Earths* which allowed their major heroes, Superman, Batman, Wonder Woman, the Flash and Green Lantern, to be 'rebooted' and modernised.

Many of the independent publishers of the Eighties had fallen by the wayside by the end of the decade.

Their other innovation, the principle of creator ownership, was taken up by a group of high-profile mainly Marvel artists who were dissatisfied with working for hire at a time when sales were booming. Marvel's 1991 *X-Men* 1 was the highest-selling comic book of all time at six million copies, although much of this was due to astute marketing – the comic came in five different interlocking covers.

A group of popular young artists including Todd McFarlane, Jim Lee and Rob Liefeld left Marvel to form their own venture, Image, and introduced a slew of new superhero comics, amongst them *Spawn, WildCATS*, and *Youngblood*. These sold in great numbers by riding the crest of the wave, but their impact was not lasting.

Boom was followed by bust as the Nineties progressed, and comic sales took a downward turn again. DC made major changes to their flagship heroes, 'killing' Superman and replacing Bruce Wayne as Batman after he suffered a broken back, although both superheroes returned to the status quo. The profusion of grim and gritty stories was eventually countered by a new trend towards 'reconstruction'. Alan Moore paid homage to early Marvel in his *1963* series for Image and then created his own line of comics under the ABC banner.

Superhero comics are today driven by 'event' storylines which run across multiple titles involving all the company's major characters in a gigantic story, usually involving an apocalyptic threat. The tendency to reboot and relaunch is still prevalent. In tandem with its regular line, Marvel created the Ultimate Universe featuring updated versions of their signature characters, beginning with Spider-Man in 2000.

The superhero remains a quintessentially American creation. Japanese manga has been a growing influence but, since the Eighties, it has been British creators who

▶ *Akira*, one of the pioneering Japanese manga style comics.

▶▶ Superheroes became even bigger business in late 2009 when the Walt Disney empire announced it was to buy Marvel Entertainment for $4bn (£2.5bn).

have mounted an invasion of the comic-book world. Some of the most sought-after and inventive writers and artists of the current century hail from the UK.

Whilst comic-book sales remained at low levels, the superhero movie came of age in the twenty-first century. Many Marvel characters made the transition to celluloid in the wake of the success of the first *X-Men* film in 2002 and the celluloid versions of Superman and

Batman were relaunched. Although this does not seem to have translated into increased sales of new superhero comics, there is a booming market for back issues; Golden Age comics and significant comics from later eras change hands for vast sums. Since the late Eighties, collections of superhero comics have been available in high-street bookshops. After 70 years and many adventures, the superhero has finally arrived in the mainstream.

The Heroes

▶ The Batmobile arrives at the UK film première of *The Dark Knight*.

From Batman to the X-Men, we profile the mythical men and women who have given so much pleasure to generations as they fight to maintain law, order and the American way of life.

Batman

Editor Vincent Sullivan gave the Bat-Man (the name was initially hyphenated), and his millionaire playboy alter ego Bruce Wayne, his debut in *Detective Comics* 27, dated May 1939. Unlike most other superheroes, the character's origin was not revealed immediately. Readers had to wait six months before discovering that, after witnessing the murder of his parents, revenge on the criminal fraternity was Batman's principal motivation.

Batman began as a lone gun-toting vigilante, equally likely to despatch villains as arrest them. The DC hierarchy was starting to adopt a more responsible editorial policy of toning down violence, particularly by heroes. Batman's modus operandi had to change. The arrival of teenage sidekick Robin in April 1940 continued the process, the ultimate expression of which was the camp Sixties television show.

Other famous elements of the Batman myth were gradually added. The utility belt arrived in his second appearance, whilst the Batmobile first hit the road in 1941, replacing his ordinary sedan car. The Batcave evolved from chambers underneath Wayne Manor which housed the

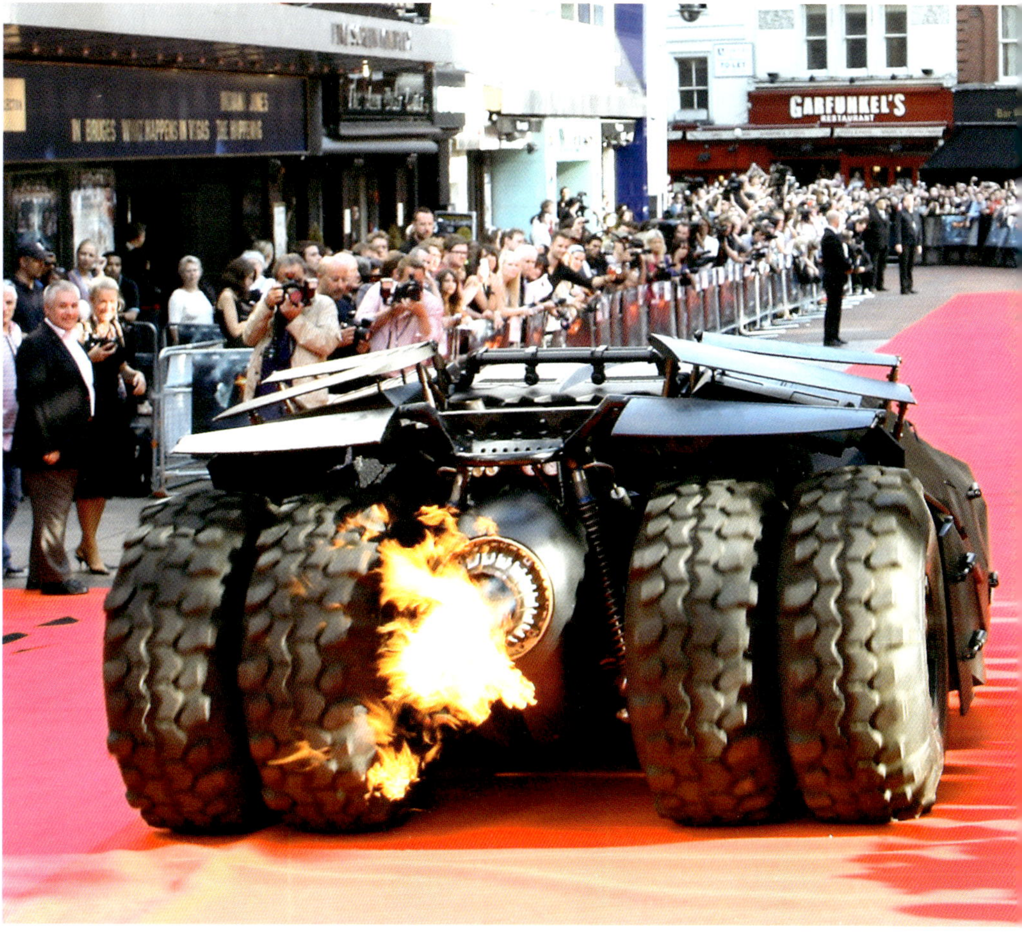
GARFUNKEL'S
RESTAURANT

Batmobile and Batplane, whilst the slightly surreal setting of Gotham City gave birth to a procession of eccentric and threatening supervillains.

Whether by accident or design, Batman was the opposite of Superman. He possessed no superpowers, just scientific knowledge, detective skills and a body trained to the peak of human ability. Superman was altruistic and dressed in primary colours, Batman the dark-clad avenger. Nevertheless, the two became friends, teaming up every month in *World's Finest Comics* and serving together in the Justice League of America. Not until Frank Miller's *The Dark Knight Returns* in 1986 was it shown how they might fare in opposition.

Reclaiming some of his gothic mystery in the late Sixties, as a reaction to the silliness of the television series, Batman has remained close to the dark side ever since.

Captain America

Captain America was created in 1941 by Joe Simon and Jack Kirby, partly as a response to the anti-war lobby in the United States. He was not the first patriotic superhero – that honour went to MLJ's the Shield – but was undoubtedly the most popular. The character's title was a best-seller, remaining so long after his creators left Timely Comics following a dispute over unpaid royalties.

Scrawny Steve Rogers attempts to enlist for the US Army and is rejected. Instead he finds himself part of a secret project led by scientist Josef Reinstein, developer of the Super Soldier serum. When administered to Rogers, the formula transforms him into 'a nearly perfect human being', with physical attributes at the peak of human potential. A Nazi spy then kills Reinstein, the only person who knows the formula, ensuring Rogers remains its only beneficiary.

Whilst his alter ego was a bumbling army private, Captain America led the superheroes into war, facing Hitler and bizarre fictional henchmen including long-term antagonist the Red Skull. Armed with his circular shield, Rogers was accompanied by a teenage sidekick, the secret-identity-free Bucky Barnes.

Apart from a brief 1954 revival, Captain America went into limbo from 1950 to 1964 when he was discovered

◀ The Caped Crusader.

▼ *Captain America*, first issue, reproduced on a stamp.

▶ Captain America disassembled by a hydra attack.

by the Avengers in a block of ice, having been in suspended animation since the end of the war. Bucky was, apparently, dead. Starring again in his own series, the character's exploits were drawn by Jack Kirby who returned to his most famous creation again in 1975 in time to celebrate the United States' bicentennial. Shortly before that Rogers, disillusioned with Watergate-era America, had renounced patriotism to become, briefly, Nomad, the man without a country. In 2007, Steve Rogers was assassinated during Marvel's Civil War storyline and replaced as Captain America by Bucky who had, it turned out, survived after all.

Captain Marvel

The first appearance of Captain Marvel was in *Whiz Comics*.

Nicknamed 'the Big Red Cheese', Captain Marvel was created by artist CC Beck and writer Bill Parker for Fawcett Publications in 1940. Their twist on the superhero formula was to make his alter ego a 12-year-old boy, Billy Batson, thus tapping into the wish-fulfilment fantasies of a young readership. Billy is given the catchphrase 'Shazam!' by a wizard of that name and, upon uttering it, a lightning bolt transforms him into Captain Marvel.

'Shazam!' is an acronym, giving the hero the wisdom of Solomon, the strength of Hercules, the stamina of Atlas, the power of Zeus, the courage of Achilles and the speed of Mercury. Saying the magic word again reverses the process. In the early Forties, the World's Mightiest Mortal, was joined by spin-off 'family' characters Mary Marvel and Captain Marvel Junior with similar costumes and powers.

In 1941, DC took legal action, alleging copyright infringement of Superman. Despite a resemblance in appearance, the two characters were very different. Captain Marvel's adventures developed into light-hearted whimsy, pitting him against non-threatening villains such as mad scientist Dr Sivana,

Captain Marvel, the most cosmic superhero of all.

who coined his nickname, and Mr Mind, an intelligent worm. Perhaps the real reason for the lawsuit was that Captain Marvel, with a circulation of almost one and a half million, was outselling Superman.

When the plagiarism case finally came to trial in 1948, Fawcett won but DC appealed. Because of the costs of legal action and the fact that the bottom had fallen out of the superhero market, Fawcett gave in and settled out of court in 1953. The Captain Marvel comics were immediately discontinued.

Marvel Comics acquired the name Captain Marvel in 1967. When DC obtained the rights to the character in 1973, it was forced to publish as *Shazam!* Ironically, in view of the character's history, Captain Marvel has become an integral part of the DC universe.

▶ Another gripping adventure for Captain Marvel.

Daredevil

Debuting in April 1964, *Daredevil – The Man Without Fear* was the last of the new wave of Marvel superheroes. An integral part of the company's style was heroes with flaws which served as a counterbalance to their superhuman abilities, ensuring they never became all-powerful, like Superman. X-Men's Professor Xavier was wheelchair-bound, Iron Man had a weak heart, Thor's alter ego was crippled and Daredevil was blind.

Surprisingly, he was not the first sightless superhero; DC's Forties character Doctor Mid-Nite had used infrared senses to compensate. Neither was he the first superhero named Daredevil – a hero of that name had been published in the Golden Age by the long-defunct Gleason. Stan Lee drew on memories of pulp tales of blind detectives and district attorneys for inspiration. Co-creator Bill Everett stayed for just one issue, whilst Daredevil's original yellow and red costume was replaced by the familiar all-red version in issue 7.

▼ Daredevil, the man without fear.

Teenager Matt Murdock was struck by a canister of radioactive material whilst saving a blind man from a runaway truck. Robbing him of his sight, the accident enhanced his other senses and gave Murdock extraordinarily acute radar, allowing him to 'see' by detecting objects around him. Armed with his billy-club, he fights crime as Daredevil and, by day, is a defence lawyer.

Daredevil was in danger of cancellation after long-term penciller Gene Colan had departed, when the largely untested artist Frank Miller began drawing it in 1979. Soon

▶ The cover of an early *Daredevil* comic.

▶▶ A *Fantastic Four* annual.

taking over as writer, Miller re-invigorated the title, reworking the hero's origin and abilities, also adding an authentic depiction of the series' gritty Hell's Kitchen setting. He introduced a new love interest in Elektra, a ninja mercenary who graduated to her own series and, in 2005, movie. His tenure catapulted Daredevil into the front rank of Marvel heroes, setting the tone for what followed and providing the basis for the 2003 film.

Fantastic Four

According to a possibly apocryphal yarn of Stan Lee's, it was during a round of golf between his boss Martin Goodman and DC publisher Jack Liebowitz that the seeds of *Fantastic Four* were sown. When Liebowitz reportedly boasted about the impressive sales figures of *Justice League of America*, Goodman wanted a piece of the action.

Both Stan Lee and Jack Kirby subsequently claimed the lion's share of the credit for creating *Fantastic Four* and debate still simmers on the subject. Theirs was not the usual writer/artist relationship; Kirby was instrumental in devising plot and characters rather than simply drawing from a script.

The original story saw the quartet stealing a prototype spaceship which was then bombarded by cosmic radiation. This transformed Reed Richards into the stretchable Mister Fantastic, Susan Storm into the

▶ A model of the Silver Surfer character.

▶▶ The Fantastic Four in the 2007 film.

Invisible Girl and Johnny Storm into the Human Torch, while Ben Grimm became the powerful but monstrous Thing.

When it appeared late in 1961, the first Marvel comic had an immediate impact. *Fantastic Four* represented a departure from traditional superhero comics: they had no secret identities, bickered constantly amongst themselves and their abilities were as much a curse as a blessing. The absence of costumes (they adopted utilitarian jumpsuits in the fourth issue) was a device to avoid competing directly in the superhero field with their distributor, DC. The inaugural villain, Mole Man, was no standard comic-book bad guy,

possessing both motivation and a tragic quality as he had been shunned by mankind because of his hideous appearance.

Lee and Kirby worked together on the first 102 issues of *Fantastic Four*, a run which contains some of the finest and most innovative superhero comics, spawning spin-off characters like the Black Panther, the Inhumans and the Silver Surfer. The relationships between the original members remain the core of Fantastic Four, something the makers of two movies in 2005 and 2007 were careful to reproduce.

▶ The Barry Allen version of Flash.

▶▶ A young boy reading about the original Flash in *Flash Comics*.

Flash

The Flash took his bow in 1940 in a story by Gardner Fox and artist Harry Lampert in which college student Jay Garrick gained his powers after inhaling hard water vapours which were said to 'make a person act much quicker than ordinary'. Donning a costume replete with cumbersome hat, his adventures ran for 11 years.

September 1956 witnessed one of the crucial moments in superhero history when, in *Showcase* 4, a new Flash, unconnected with the previous incarnation, was unleashed. Police scientist Barry Allen was performing a chemical experiment when the lab was struck by lightning. This combined with the chemicals to give him super speed. The only link between the two characters was that Allen adopted the name of a superhero whose exploits he recalled reading as a child, kick-starting the second coming of the superhero. The revival was the brainchild of editor Julius Schwartz, and was realised by writer Robert Khaniger and artist Carmine Infantino, who later became DC's publisher.

The Flash returned to his own comic with issue 105, continuing the old numbering to save money. Another milestone was reached in issue 123 when the new Flash met his Golden Age counterpart. That September 1961 story inaugurated DC's increasingly convoluted series of parallel worlds, explaining that their Golden Age heroes actually existed on Earth-Two.

By 1985, things were so complicated that a clean-up operation, *Crisis On Infinite Earths*, was staged. The progenitor of company-wide event stories, it collapsed all alternate realities into one, allowing DC to reboot their major heroes. The Barry Allen Flash died during the series and his mantle was taken by Wally West, aka his former sidekick Kid Flash.

It was the Barry Allen version of the character who appeared in CBS's television version of *The Flash*, which lasted for one season only. Meanwhile, in the comics, Allen has returned from the dead...

DC
DECEMBER
FLASH COMICS
No. 102
HAWKMAN
The FLYING BUBBLES!

Green Lantern

Three years after the debut of the Silver Age Flash, Julius Schwartz masterminded the revival of another Forties hero. Originally created in 1940 by artist Martin Nodell, the character of Green Lantern was fleshed out by writer Bill Finger at editor Sheldon Mayer's

▶ A *Green Lantern* comic cover.

▶▶ A 2009 *Green Lantern* comic.

▶▶▶ A poster for the *Green Lantern* animated film.

request. Alan Scott finds a magic lantern and discovers that, when touched, a ring made of the lantern's material gives him superpowers. Clad in a costume of clashing colours, he fought evil as Green Lantern until 1949.

Like the Flash, Green Lantern was given a complete makeover, including a sleeker outfit designed by artist Gil

Kane. The new adventures were written by John Broome who introduced a science-fiction element to the mix. Test pilot Hal Jordan is given a lantern, battery and power ring by a dying alien who represents an outer space police force, the Green Lantern Corps. The power wielded by the hero was almost infinite – he could affect people's minds, create objects out of nothing and turn back missiles. As a counterbalance, two limitations were devised: the ring would not work against anything coloured yellow and its battery had to be recharged every 24 hours.

The hero's dwindling popularity led to a change of direction in 1970 when Green Lantern was teamed up with Green Arrow, the marksman hero who had recently received a makeover courtesy of writer Denny O'Neil and artist Neal Adams. They were also responsible for the landmark 'relevant' storyline teaming the anti-establishment Green Arrow with the arch-conservative Green Lantern.

In later years when Hal Jordan became Parallax and went to explore the universe, others took on the role of Green Lantern – Guy Gardner, John Stewart and Kyle Rayner – but Jordan has since returned as a member of the Green Lantern Corps.

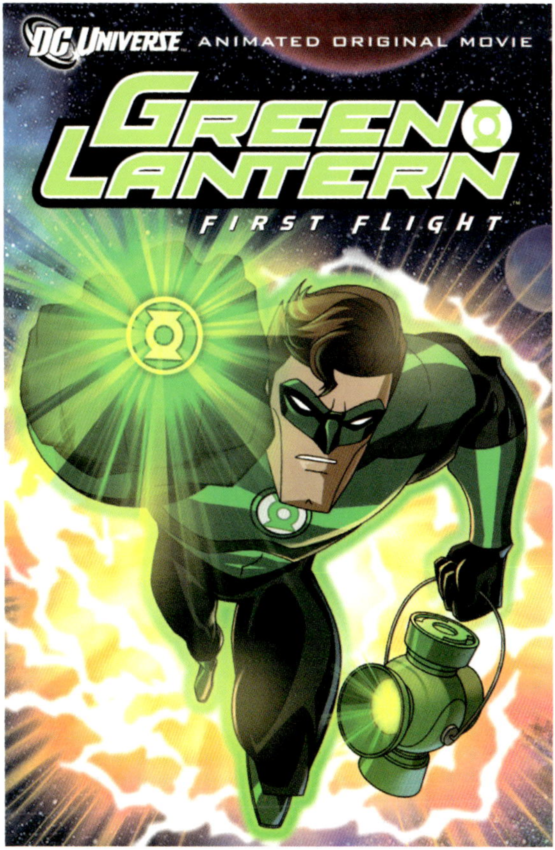

Human Torch

Early superhero comics were often created and packaged by studios and sold to publishers. Martin Goodman's Timely began in this way before the publisher opted to bring editorial control in-house. *Marvel Comics* 1 (November 1939) was the work of Funnies Inc, run by Lloyd Jacquet. Two of the characters featured in that issue, the Sub-Mariner and the Human Torch, were hits and would enjoy long runs even though their appearance on the cover of the comic was noticeably different to that inside.

Written and drawn by Carl Burgos, the Human Torch was an android built by Professor Phineas T Horton which accidentally burst into flames when exposed to oxygen. The sentient robot rebelled against his creator, was imprisoned underground but broke free, inadvertently setting fire to parts of New York. Ultimately, the Torch learnt to control his flammability and decided to put it to use helping humanity. He was later joined by

▶ The Human Torch fighting Japanese.

▶▶ The Human Torch defeats a villain.

teenage sidekick Toro, a mutant whose exposure to radiation gave him similar flaming abilities.

The obvious although probably unplanned clash of the elements fire and water led to the first crossover in comics when a confrontation between the Torch and the Sub-Mariner took up the whole of *Marvel Mystery Comics* 9. The Human Torch began appearing in his own title in 1940. The Torch's adventures ended in 1949 as superheroes fell from favour at the end of the Second World War, although the character underwent a brief revival in 1953-54.

Fantastic Four's Human Torch was unrelated to the original who cropped up as a villain in 1965. His body was thought to have been used to create the Avengers' synthetic superhero the Vision in 1968, but this theory was revised in the Eighties when the original Torch returned to become a member of the Avengers west-coast offshoot, demonstrating once again that, in superhero comics, things are rarely as they seem.

Incredible Hulk

Marvel's second superhero was not, initially a hit. The Hulk's original 1962 title was cancelled after six issues as its sales were insufficient to merit a place in the company's restricted distribution schedule. The character was, however, kept alive by guest appearances in other comics until an ongoing series was revived in *Tales To Astonish*.

The influences behind the character's creation lay in the combination of Jack Kirby's interest in people showing unusual strength at times of great stress and Stan Lee's fascination for the monsters in *The Hunchback Of Notre Dame*, *Frankenstein* and *Dr Jekyll And Mr Hyde*. Another factor was the company's background in monster stories, the influence of which also lingered in *Fantastic Four*'s the Thing. The Hulk, however, represented a more radical departure for superhero comics, featuring the monster in the starring role.

Like many Marvel characters, the Hulk's origin story was rooted in cold-war paranoia and fears about the effects of atomic radiation. Scientist Bruce

▶ The Incredible Hulk at Madame Tussauds.

▶▶ A red Hulk.

Banner is caught in the blast from an experimental 'Gamma Bomb' whilst saving a teenage boy from it. Later, this transforms him into a hugely powerful green-skinned creature. Although the change was eventually triggered by Banner's fear or anger, it took various creators a while to arrive at this via several false starts, including initially, the Hulk emerging at onset of darkness.

The early Hulk also experienced

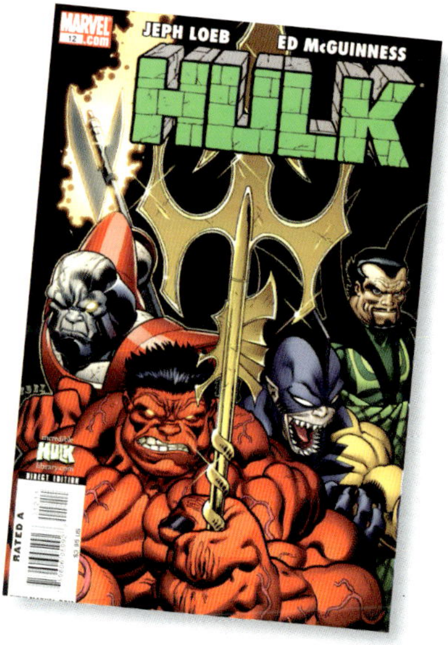

fluctuations in his character before becoming angry, monosyllabic and rather stupid. At various points in his history, Banner has gained and lost control of the Hulk. In later years, the variations on the character have been explained as a multiple personality disorder. As two movies and a television series have shown, the Hulk is difficult to recreate convincingly on screen. Nevertheless he continues to loom as large as ever on the page.

▶ The Hulk shows his incredible power.

▶▶ A cover battle between Tony Stark and archrival Obediah Stane.

Iron Man

The expanding Marvel universe had its fair share of technological geniuses – Fantastic Four's Reed Richards, villain Dr Doom and the Hulk's alter ego Bruce Banner. They were joined in March 1963 by Tony Stark, the millionaire playboy

inventor who became Iron Man.

The character was masterminded by Stan Lee, who assigned his brother Larry Lieber to script the first issue, designed by Jack Kirby and drawn by another veteran artist, Don Heck. The

▲ One of a series of stamps celebrating *Marvel Comics*.

▶ Another thrilling episode in the life of Iron Man.

original tale had an unusually political tone, which Lee later regretted. The action takes place in Vietnam where Stark is testing his new weaponry for the US Army. Injured in an attack which lodges a piece of shrapnel near his heart and captured by the Viet Cong, the inventor is put to work devising weapons for the enemy. With the help of a Vietnamese boffin, he creates a suit of armour containing a breastplate designed to prevent the shrapnel from reaching his heart and killing him. The suit gives him superhuman strength and is equipped with powerful 'repulsor rays', fired from the

palms of the hand.

The original bulky grey Iron Man armour became gold in his second appearance but was soon replaced altogether by a sleeker red and gold version which proved more enduring. Tony Stark's life was given a touch of melodrama by the need to periodically recharge the breastplate to stay alive. The hero's alter ego was based on Howard Hughes and Lee claimed that the character was most popular amongst Marvel's female readers. Eventually, Stark was fitted with an artificial heart but he then descended into a long battle with alcoholism.

Subsequent re-imaginings of the hero's origin have eschewed the Cold War anti-Communist angle, replacing it with more contemporary themes of terrorism and corporate crime. The 2008 movie, starring Robert Downey Jr – a fan of the comic book – relocated the setting to Afghanistan.

◀ Robert Downey Jr., the latest incarnation of Iron Man.

▶ The first issue of the recently updated *Justice League of America*.

▶▶ The Justice League's main protaganists.

Justice Society of America and Justice League of America

The first team of superheroes, the Justice Society of America, made its debut in winter 1940 in *All Star Comics* 3. The originator of the concept is unknown although Sheldon Mayer, Gardner Fox and Maxwell Gaines are the prime suspects. The Justice Society represented an attempt by DC's sister company, All-American, to come up with a blockbuster to match Superman and Batman. Whilst it never reached those heights, the basic idea of a super team was an enduring one.

Strangely, the Justice Society's members rarely operated together as the stories began and ended with a meeting, whilst in-between times the individual superheroes starred in separate chapters. The founders were Flash, Green Lantern, Hawkman, the Atom, Dr Fate, Hourman and Sandman, Wonder Woman joined later, whilst Superman and Batman were honorary members who only made a couple of appearances. Like many other superheroes, the Society's run ended in the early Fifties.

Nine years later, Julius Schwartz revived the notion, substituted the 'League' for the outdated 'Society' and assigned Gardner Fox, veteran scribe of the Justice Society, to pen the new version which was drawn by crowd-scene expert Mike Sekowsky. Initially, Superman and Batman took a back seat, leaving Martian Manhunter, Aquaman, Wonder Woman, Flash and Green Lantern to tackle the villains. This they often did in pairs, presumably to reduce congestion. The team's reader identification character, finger-clicking teenage sidekick 'Snapper' Carr, proved irritating and was written out after 77 issues.

After a try-out in *The Brave And The Bold*, the JLA graduated to their own comic, the success of which influenced the re-entry of Marvel Comics into the superhero field with *Fantastic Four*. Marvel eventually came up with their own version of the Justice League, the Avengers in 1964, while the original Justice Society made a brief comeback in the mid-Seventies.

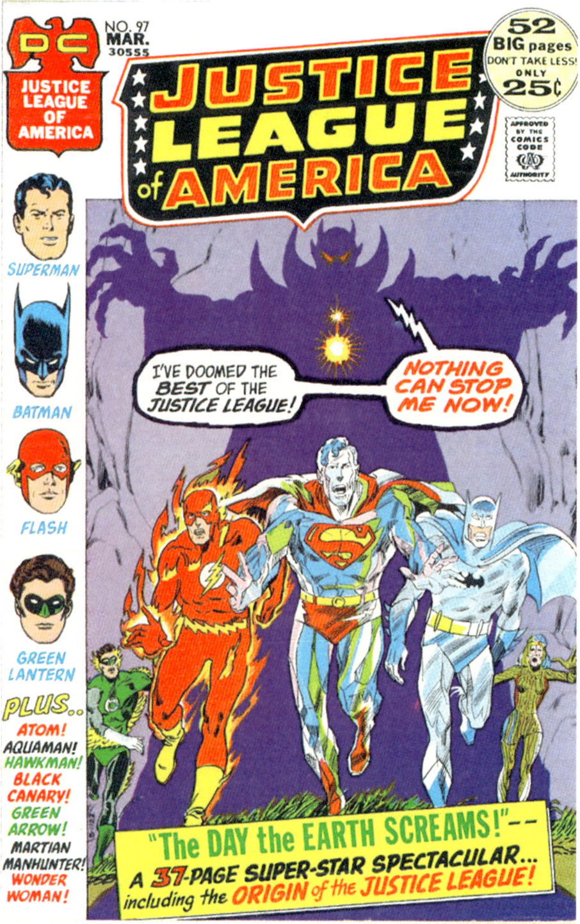

Marvelman/ Miracleman

When Fawcett cancelled their *Captain Marvel* comics in 1953, London publishers L Miller & Sons were left without material for their popular line of British reprints. They called in comics packager Mick Anglo who reworked the character into Marvelman. In the new version, reporter Mickey Moran becomes Marvelman on speaking the magic word 'Kimota!' (phonetically, 'atomic' backwards). He was joined by sidekicks Young Marvelman and Kid Marvelman. The heroes' appearances closely resembled those of the originals whilst the numbering of the comics continued. They ceased publication in 1963.

Believing the copyright to be in the public domain, editor Dez Skinn revived Marvelman for *Warrior* in March 1982, assigning Alan Moore as writer and Garry Leach as artist. Moore took superheroes into new territory, along the way explaining the origins of the Marvelman family as the product of alien body-swapping technology. Marvelman's last appearance in *Warrior* was in August 1984 due to creative differences between Moore and artist Alan Davis. Since the original character's final outing, Marvel Comics

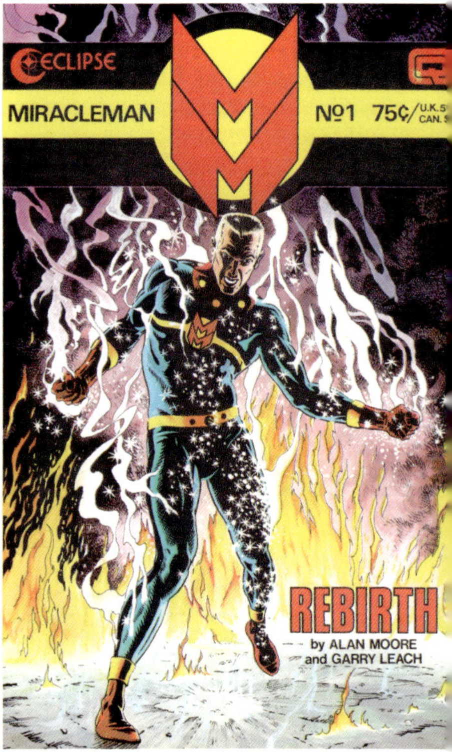

▶ The first issue of revived *Miracleman*.

▶▶ Eclipse Comics issue 6 is the first *Miracleman* with new material.

to *Miracleman* for its American publication by independent Eclipse in 1985. In 1989, Moore was succeeded as writer by Neil Gaiman who worked with Mark Buckingham as artist. Eclipse went bankrupt in 1993, ending the comic's run with issue 24.

The uncertain issue of ownership of the character was further complicated when Image partner Todd McFarlane purchased the rights to Eclipse's properties in 1994. Gaiman challenged his ownership of Miracleman, arguing that the character belonged to him. The situation was unresolved despite a court hearing in the States but in July 2009, Marvel Comics

had become an established international brand and the company's threats of legal action forced a name change

announced that it had purchased the rights to the character from original creator Mick Anglo.

Spider-Man

Sporting a colourful costume and hiding a secret identity, Spider-Man was, at first glance, a more traditional superhero than Fantastic Four and Hulk – but the series also contained elements which set Marvel apart from their competitors. As teenager Peter Parker, the hero was beset by money problems, and troubles with girls, and was forever worried about his ailing Aunt May. Spider-Man meanwhile was hounded by the police and regularly denounced as a menace by newspaper tycoon J Jonah Jameson.

The character's genesis remains the subject of controversy. Stan Lee has variously stated that he was inspired by watching a spider spinning a web and by the pulp character the Spider. Others maintain that Jack Kirby developed the idea of a spider-powered hero with Joe Simon and suggested it to Lee. Believing

▶ Spider-Man, one of the most successful comic characters of all time.

▶▶ The rare first issue of *The Amazing Spider-Man* comic.

Kirby's art to be too heroic for his realistic conception of Spider-Man, Lee replaced him with Steve Ditko whose detailed, slightly creepy style fitted the strip perfectly.

Publisher Martin Goodman objected that people don't like spiders and the series made a low-key debut in *Amazing Fantasy* 15, the final issue. Lee claims that he could only persuade his reluctant boss to run Spider-Man in a comic which was about to be cancelled. Lee also maintained that positive reader reaction resulted in the character being launched in his own title, *The Amazing Spider-Man*, in 1963.

▶ Marvel's Spider-Man.

Ditko's replacement, John Romita, drew Spider-Man in a more conventionally heroic manner and the comic became Marvel's best-seller, a position it held until overhauled by *X-Men* in the Eighties.

Spider-Man has evolved over the years – leaving school, getting married and controversially changing his red and blue costume for an all-black number, although this turned out to be alien supervillain Venom. Like many of Marvel's superhero movies, the *Spider-Man* series successfully balanced an update on the character's origin whilst retaining the essence of the comic.

Spirit

The Spirit is the most famous creation of one of the most influential figures in American comics' history, Will Eisner. One of superhero comics' earliest entrepreneurs, Eisner formed a comic-book packaging studio with Jerry Iger in 1938. His first superhero, Amazing Man, was abruptly terminated by DC's legal action; Eisner testified in court that he had been asked to copy Superman. More lasting characters originated by Eisner included Doll Man, Uncle Sam, Black Condor and Blackhawk.

In 1940, publisher 'Busy' Arnold came up with the idea of supplying

The crime-fighting superhero, Spirit.

newspapers with a weekly comic-book section and commissioned Eisner to create the main feature and package the remainder. The Spirit was a combination of superheroics and detective fiction. Private eye Denny Colt was pursuing the villainous Dr Cobra when he fell into a vat of chemicals and was presumed dead. Two days later, a masked man appeared at the office of Police Commissioner Dolan, revealed himself to be Denny Colt and vowed to fight crime in the guise of the Spirit whilst remaining officially dead and living under Wildwood Cemetery. Eisner sold his interest in the studio to concentrate on producing the weekly strip which he did until 1951, with some assistance from colleagues particularly during his national service.

▶ An early issue of *The Spirit*.

The innovative layouts and storytelling techniques used by Eisner on the Spirit were massively influential on succeeding generations of superhero artists. Eisner also coined the term 'graphic novel' for comics published in book form.

The Spirit was almost unique in early comics in that Eisner retained copyright to his character and was able to profit from its continued popularity as it was spun-off into comic books, magazines and a series of deluxe reprints produced under DC's aegis. The company also produced new Spirit material following Eisner's death in 2004. A Frank Miller-directed movie was released in 2008.

Sub-Mariner

The first true antihero in superhero comics was the Sub-Mariner, although Batman initially trod a morally ambivalent path. The character made his first appearance in *Motion Picture Funnies*, a cinema giveaway produced by Funnies Inc. When a better deal came along from Timely, Sub-Mariner was dusted off for inclusion in the first issue of *Marvel Comics*.

Sub-Mariner's creator/writer/artist Bill Everett could trace his family ancestry back to visionary poet William Blake. A further link to English poetry was provided by Everett's statement that his character was partly inspired by Coleridge's *The Rime Of The Ancient Mariner*.

The Sub-Mariner, Prince Namor, was the product of a liaison between a princess of an undersea kingdom and

A preliminary design for an American stamp featuring the Sub-Mariner.

▶ Namor, the Sub-Mariner.

▶▶ The Superman logo.

an American sea captain conducting an expedition in the area. In the Sixties the kingdom was identified as Atlantis. Namor's hybrid nature gave him extraordinary strength, endurance and stamina, qualities not actually possessed by either race. He also had the equally inexplicable ability to fly. Much later, his powers were explained as the product of mutation.

Seeking vengeance on the surface world for its attacks on his people, Namor subsequently put aside his differences to fight against the Axis powers in the Second World War. Disappearing shortly after the end of the war, the character was revived in 1962 in *Fantastic Four* when Johnny Storm, the new Human Torch, found him living as a derelict in New York. This confirmed that the new Marvel superheroes existed in the same fictional universe as their wartime counterparts.

Namor's role as antihero continued as he plagued the Fantastic Four occasionally teamed up with Dr Doom and the Hulk. His own series, which began in 1965, saw Sub-Mariner on a quest to find his people who had relocated because of nuclear testing. The character remains an important part of the Marvel universe.

Superman

There can be few people on the planet unaware of the 'Man of Steel' who, as an infant boy, was dispatched in a spaceship from doomed planet Krypton. The lesser gravity of Earth gave him superhuman abilities like being able to leap tall buildings in a single bound; the rest is history...

Like many revolutionary notions, Jerry Siegel and Joe Shuster's groundbreaking character was not picked up immediately and went unpublished for five years. Even when it was accepted for the first issue of *Action Comics* in June 1938, DC publisher Harry Donenfeld almost vetoed the iconic cover because it showed Superman doing the impossible, lifting a car over his head.

▶ Christopher Reeve as Superman.

Superman defined the genre from the start, establishing the superhero as a costumed adventurer with extraordinary abilities and a secret, civilian identity. The first story introduced a bizarre love triangle with feisty reporter Lois Lane falling in love with Superman but having only contempt for his alter ego, Clark Kent. Lois's attitude to Kent would soften over the years and she would, like teenage reporter Jimmy Olsen, star in her own comic book, part of a growing range of Superman-related titles.

Superman was inspired by a combination of ancient mythology, science fiction, pulp heroes and Philip Wylie's 1930 novel *Gladiator*. The awkward, bespectacled Clark Kent was based on Siegel and Shuster themselves. Superman's powers evolved into flight, X-ray vision, heat and ice breath, and eventually the ability to push planets around in space.

DC continuity had it that the original Superman lived on Earth-Two and that his counterpart on the 'real' world, Earth Prime, had arrived in the Sixties. After the company eradicated its complicated system of parallel worlds, writer/artist John Byrne remodelled the character in 1986. The character has since died and been resurrected. The subject of numerous big and small-screen interpretations, Superman will undoubtedly live forever.

◀ The latest capeless Superman who has had to adjust to married life.

Thor

Superheroes – Wonder Woman and Captain Marvel in particular – had acknowledged their heritage in ancient mythology before, but in 1962, when Stan Lee was searching for a way to up the ante after the creation of the Hulk, he decided to use a bona fide mythological god as a character. Coincidentally, Jack Kirby had featured Norse deity Thor as a villain in the Forties.

Crippled physician Donald Blake is holidaying in Norway when he finds a gnarled stick in a cave. By striking it against a wall, he is transformed into the Mighty Thor and the stick into the enchanted hammer Mjolinor, which bears the inscription "Whosoever wields this hammer, if he be worthy, shall possess the power of Thor."

Other elements of the Norse pantheon were introduced – Loki, the god of mischief, became Thor's most persistent antagonist and Asgard, home of the gods, was depicted as a city floating in space. The series really began to take off when Kirby concentrated on a handful of comics rather than spreading

▶ The mighty Thor.

▶▶ The first appearance of Thor.

▶▶▶ The Viking based hero in action.

himself thinly across the line. This allowed his artwork and plotting to reach new heights. For his part, Lee adopted a cod-Shakespearean approach for the Norse Gods dialogue, peppering it with 'thees' and 'thous'. As in *Fantastic Four*, they combined cosmic adventure with earthly melodrama.

As the mythological background assumed greater importance, an explanation for the existence of Donald Blake had to be found. It emerged that Odin had exiled the arrogant Thor to Earth in the form of a crippled doctor to teach him humility. Eventually, the Blake persona was phased out.

In 1983, writer/artist Walt Simonson gave the series a new lease of life when an alien warrior, Beta Ray Bill, briefly became Thor, fulfilling the legend of the hammer. The hero also gained a new alter ego, Eric Masterson. Thor was revamped and updated in 2000 as Donald Blake returned.

Wonder Woman

Wonder Woman was created in 1941 as reaction to the 'blood-curdling masculinity', of superheroes. William Marston, psychiatrist and developer of the polymath lie detector, had written articles critical of comics, leading to an invitation to sit on DC/All-American's editorial advisory board and subsequently to submit ideas for characters. Utilising his knowledge of mythology, he devised Wonder Woman.

US pilot Steve Trevor crash-lands on remote Paradise Island, home of the Amazons whose queen decides to find a champion to return with Trevor and fight the Nazis.

▶ Superman and Wonder Woman flying together.

▶▶ Lynda Carter portrayed Wonder Woman on TV.

The ensuing tournament is won, incognito, by her daughter Diana who was forbidden to enter. Armed with bullet-deflecting bracelets, truth-compelling Magic Lasso and villain-reforming Venus Girdle, Diana is given a costume suspiciously similar to the American flag. Stateside, she adopts the identity of nurse Diana Prince.

Original artist Harry Peter was thought to be nearly 60 when Marston chose him to illustrate Wonder Woman. His art-deco influenced style lent the early adventures a distinctive atmosphere. Marston sparked controversy with frequent depictions of bondage; fortunately the details of his home life, where he lived in a polygamous relationship with two women, were not publicly known.

Subsequent creative

teams kept the character alive, pandering to the romance genre in the Fifties and succumbing to whimsy in the Sixties. In 1970, the ailing title was given a makeover when Wonder Woman lost her powers to become a karate-kicking, cat-suited heroine in the mould of Emma Peel from British television's *The Avengers*. Under pressure from feminist Gloria Steinem, DC reversed the changes in 1973.

Wonder Woman was sympathetically reinvented by writer/artist George Pérez in 1987. Before that, the statuesque Lynda Carter made her name bringing the heroine to life on television for three seasons between 1975 and 1978.

With a publishing pedigree of more than 65 years, Wonder Woman remains the doyen of superheroines, a feminist icon in a field traditionally dominated by males.

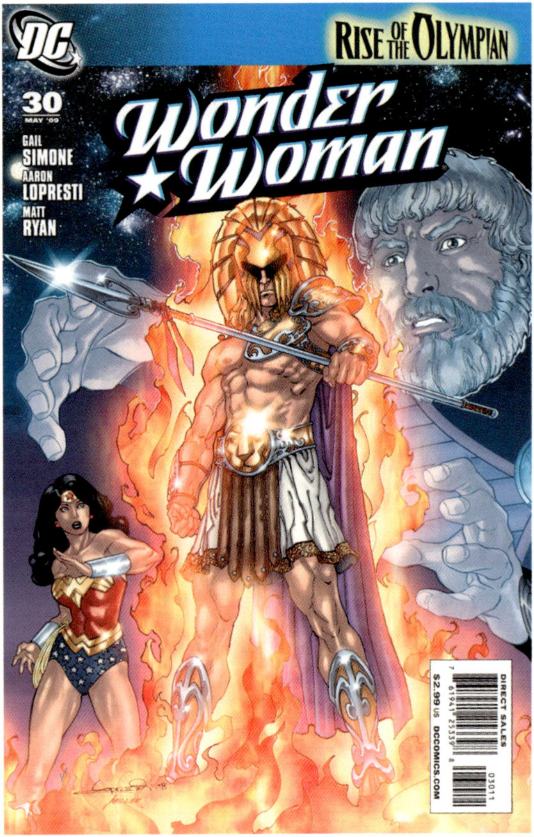

▶ Wonder Woman continues to be popular.

▶▶ The X-Men featured on a stamp.

X-Men

Perhaps the slowest-burning success story in comics, X-Men were created by Stan Lee and Jack Kirby in 1963 but never rose above second division status during Marvel's early years. The concept of genetic mutants, or 'homo superior', as superheroes cleverly allowed their creators to dispense with contrived origin stories, and the anti-mutant plotlines served as a neat allegory for racial conflict.

X-Men were originally a group of teenagers assembled by wheelchair-bound Professor Charles Xavier, a powerful telepath, at his School for Gifted Youngsters in upstate New York. Mutant superpowers manifested in adolescence, mirroring the physical changes taking place at

that time whilst allowing for plenty of teenage angst. The original line-up of Cyclops, Iceman, the Beast, Angel and Marvel Girl were frequently pitted against Magneto and his Brotherhood of Evil Mutants.

Despite boasting the talents of Sixties superstar artists Jim Steranko and Neal Adams, the *X-Men* comic was discontinued in 1970 because of poor sales. Five years later, the concept was revived by editor Roy Thomas, writer Len Wein and artist Dave Cockrum with an international slant. Of the new team, borderline psychopath Wolverine was to prove most popular. When Wein's assistant, London-born Chris Claremont, assumed the writing duties soon afterwards, *X-Men* began to gain a following, building momentum when Canadian penciller John Byrne, also British-born, arrived late in 1977.

In the Eighties, *X-Men* became the company's best-seller, spawning a family of *X-Books* beginning when Wolverine span off into a solo series. Claremont developed into Marvel's most important writer since Stan Lee, staying with the comic for 16 years and reaching a sales peak with artist Jim Lee. Amongst Claremont's successors were Scottish scribe Grant Morrison and *Buffy The Vampire Slayer* creator Joss Whedon. 2000's *X-Men* movie became the first convincing big-screen adaptation of Marvel superheroes; like the comic, it generated a money-spinning franchise.

▶ Chris Claremont.

◀ Hugh Jackman in the 2000 film of *X-Men*.

The Supervillains

▶ Detail of the costume worn by Michelle Pfeiffer in the movie *Batman Returns*.

Every superhero needs an adversary. This is a rundown of the biggest baddies of the comic world, many of whom gathered cult followings of their own.

Catwoman

Catwoman's iconic status is largely due to the procession of actresses who memorably donned the Catsuit onscreen. Julie Newmar's sexily purring portrayal in the 1966 *Batman* television series put the character on the map. Newmar's unavailability meant she was replaced by Eartha Kitt for the show's third season and by Lee Meriwether in the 1966 *Batman* spin-off movie. Michelle Pfeiffer romanced Bruce Wayne as a blonde Catwoman in 1992's *Batman Returns* where she literally had nine lives. The character played by Halle Berry in the disappointing *Catwoman* (2004) had nothing to do with previous incarnations – or, indeed, the Batman mythology.

During her comic-book career, Catwoman varied between villain, reformed villain and antihero. Her debut in the first issue of Batman's own comic book established her as socialite Selina Kyle, who is also the whip-wielding thief known as the Cat. The costume she adopted to become Catwoman included a cowl which echoed Batman's. Her role as *femme fatale* was evident from the start, as was Batman's guilty fascination for her. After renouncing crime to help Batman for a while in the early Fifties,

▶ Lee Meriwether in the first Batman film.

Selina explained that her wicked ways were due to a blow on the head suffered during a plane crash, although she subsequently claimed to have invented the story. Afterwards, her motivation was ascribed partly to an abusive marriage, something expanded upon in modern Catwoman stories.

After 12 years in comic-book limbo, Catwoman's return in 1966 was the direct result of the character's appearances on television. During the Eighties, she and Batman finally became lovers for a short while. Writer Frank Miller and artist David Mazzucchelli reinvented her in 1986's *Batman: Year One*, and she was subsequently given her own title. Since then she has become a permanent fixture of the DC universe, assuming the role of antihero.

Darkseid

Whilst working on Thor at Marvel, Jack Kirby conceived the idea of killing off the hero, along with his Norse compatriots at Ragnarok, the final battle foretold in mythology, and replacing them with a new race of gods. The company, however, was understandably reluctant to lose one of its major properties, so Kirby, nearing the end of his contract with Marvel and determined not to create any new concepts or characters for them, kept the idea in reserve.

At DC in 1971, Kirby dusted off the idea for what soon became known as the *Fourth World*, a family of comic books based on a new mythology of his own invention. The villain was Darkseid whose scheming presence united the four titles – *Superman's Pal Jimmy Olsen*, *New Gods*, *Forever People* and *Mister Miracle*. After the old gods were destroyed, two new planets rose from the ashes of the conflict; the idyllic New Genesis, home of the superhero gods and Apokolips, the hell world ruled by Darkseid.

▼ The great villain, Darkseid.

▶ Darkseid.

major weapon is the Omega Effect, a beam he shoots from his eyes. This is capable of anything from stunning a victim to transforming them or obliterating them completely. His appearance is said to have been based on actor Jack Palance and his character on disgraced US President Richard Nixon.

The *Fourth World* comics were prematurely cancelled but, when Kirby returned to DC in the mid-Eighties, he fashioned a conclusion to the saga. Mindful of Darkseid's status as an iconic villain and potential for future use, the company refused to allow the character's creator to kill him off. Darkseid has since returned on numerous occasions and ranks as one of comics' greatest supervillains.

A schemer and manipulator, Darkseid was initially concerned with unlocking the Anti-Life Equation which would give him dominion over all living beings in the universe. Virtually immortal and almost invulnerable, Darkseid's

Doctor Doom

The Fantastic Four's most persistent antagonist made his first appearance in the fifth issue of the comic book in a tale which involved travelling into the past in Doctor Doom's time machine. The story revealed that Victor von Doom was a college contemporary of Reed Richards, Mr Fantastic. Von Doom's dabbling in black magic resulted in his face being horribly scarred in an accident, hence the iron mask. Two years later, this was amended to a more science-related mishap at which Reed Richards was present.

Doom's roots as an Eastern European gypsy were revealed, as well as perhaps the most interesting innovation – his status as absolute monarch of tiny Balkan principality Latveria which gave him diplomatic immunity. Re-workings of the Fantastic Four's origins, such as the movie version, have tied von Doom more closely with the accident which created the team.

Creators Stan Lee and Jack Kirby had differing visions of Doom. As far as the

▼ Dr Doom with other Marvel villains.

▲ Dr Doom and a Master of Evil.

that the injuries were slight but Doom's vanity would not allow for anything other than perfection.

Doctor Doom has had countless run-ins with the Fantastic Four. Early encounters saw him teaming up with the Sub-Mariner, stealing the Silver Surfer's powers and imprisoning the heroes in Latveria in homage to *The Prisoner* television series. In keeping with the notion of a shared universe he has battled many other Marvel superheroes, an apparent mismatch with Spider-Man included. He featured in a short-lived series of his own in 1969 and combined again with the Sub-Mariner in the mid-Seventies in *Supervillain Team Up*.

The character's introduction, in 1962, represented a conscious attempt by Lee and Kirby to develop a villain worthy of their new super team and they certainly succeeded in creating a truly iconic bad guy.

former was concerned the character's face was scarred beyond recognition in the accident. Kirby, however, maintained

Doctor Octopus and Green Goblin

A strong animal theme ran through Spider-Man's early foes with weird, highly visual characters like the Vulture, the Lizard, the Beetle, the Jackal, the Rhino and the big game-hunter Kraven. The theme continued with one of Stan Lee's favourite villains, Doctor Octopus, who first appeared in the third issue of *Spider-Man* in 1963. Forty years later the character was brought to life in *Spider-Man* 2 by Alfred Molina. Portly, bespectacled scientist Otto Octavius was experimenting with a multi-armed harness which allowed him to handle dangerous chemicals safely when an accident fused the device to his body. As Doctor Octopus, he fought Spider-Man numerous times, even succeeding in unmasking him once. He was woven into the soap opera of the strip when he courted Peter Parker's Aunt May; they were on the verge of tying the knot when the service was interrupted.

Spider-Man's foe in the first movie, portrayed by Willem Dafoe was Green Goblin, another Lee/Ditko era villain. His identity remained a mystery until

▼ Spider-Man with his enemy, Dr Octopus.

Ditko left the series. It is unlikely that the artist would have gone along with the revelation that the Goblin was Norman Osborn, an industrialist working on a super-strength formula which exploded in his face, creating the deranged villain. Osborn was the father of Parker's best friend and college roommate Harry Osborn.

Flying around on a glider and launching 'pumpkin bombs' at his enemy, the original Green Goblin was responsible for the death of Parker's girlfriend Gwen Stacy in 1973. The Goblin himself died shortly afterwards, but both he and Gwen would be resurrected, the mantle of the Goblin passing to Harry and various others. For a time, the character was superseded by the Hobgoblin.

If the mettle of a superhero can be tested by the quality of his enemies, then Spider-Man has earned his spurs the hard way.

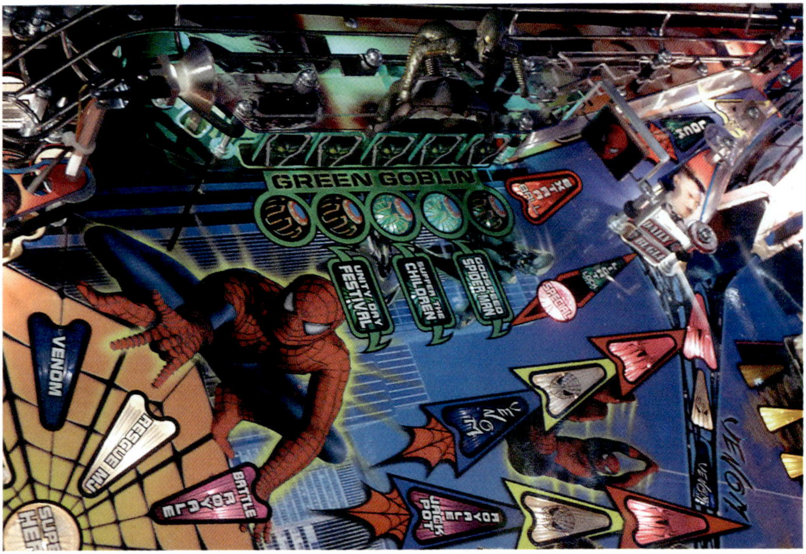

▶ Green Goblin and Spider-Man feature in a pinball machine.

▶▶ Galactus, one of the most feared beings in the cosmos.

Galactus

The mid-Sixties *Fantastic Four* contained some all-time classic superhero material. The creative team of writer Stan Lee and artist Jack Kirby were at their peak with new ideas, concepts and characters leaping off the page with every issue. Kirby was devising most of the plots, sometimes with input from Lee who added dialogue and captions, following the artist's notes on the original pages of art. Occasionally, to Kirby's annoyance, he deviated from them and altered the story, contributing to the eventual breakdown of the relationship.

Galactus' first appearance in *Fantastic Four* 48 resulted from a suggestion of Lee's that the team should meet God. That was beyond the pale for comic books in 1966 and the idea mutated into the virtually all-powerful planet-devouring entity Galactus. Needing to consume the energy of entire worlds to survive, the god-like being decides that the Earth

▶ Galactus has scientific knowledge beyond human understanding.

▶▶ The Joker with a large tattoo on his back.

▶▶▶ Jack Nicholson in front of a poster showing him as The Joker.

will be his next meal – the Fantastic Four have to stop him.

The supervillain stakes were raised to an unprecedented degree with the creation of Galactus. The character was portrayed as existing beyond good and evil, prepared to extinguish the human race as we might step on an anthill.

Dubbed the 'Galactus trilogy', *Fantastic Four* 48-50 also contained the debut of the Silver Surfer, Galactus' herald who turns on his master. This was an enduring Kirby creation which Lee would later assume control of, turning him into a tragic, Christ-like figure rather than the entirely synthetic creature who learns to be human which Kirby had initially envisaged.

Despite vowing to leave Earth alone, Galactus would return many times. The second Fantastic Four movie, *The Rise Of The Silver Surfer,* was based on the original trilogy – but instead of depicting Galactus as the giant humanoid of the comics, the producers showed the character as a cloud of cosmic matter with just a hint of his physical appearance.

Joker

The Joker is perhaps the most notorious comic-book villain of all. His bizarre appearance and eccentric modus operandi set the standard for the many grotesque villains like the Riddler, the Penguin and Two-Face who followed him into Batman's Rogue's Gallery.

Artist Bob Kane, writer Bill Finger and Kane's assistant Jerry Robinson all claimed to have created the Joker; what is certain is that the character's look was based on the playing card left as a calling card at crime scenes. Other influences

were actor Conrad Veidt in the 1928 silent film *The Man Who Laughs* and odd-looking villains Pruneface and Flattop Jones from the *Dick Tracy* newspaper strip. At the end of his second story in *Batman* 1, the Joker was slated to die until editor Whitney Ellsworth recognised his potential and reprieved him by substituting a new final panel, marking the first of countless occasions on which the character cheated death.

The Joker's green hair, white face and red lips went unexplained until

▲ Robin, Batman and The Joker in the 1960s TV series.

▶ Lex Luthor, arch enemy of Superman.

11 years after his 1940 debut. It was revealed that he was originally known as the Red Hood, the leader of a criminal gang who fell into a vat containing chemicals. The disfiguring accident is believed to have driven him insane. This was expanded upon in Alan Moore and Brian Bolland's *Batman: The Killing Joke* in 1988.

Screen interpretations of the Joker have ranged from the relatively playful Cesar Romero in the Sixties television show, to the murderously psychotic Jack Nicholson in 1989's *Batman* and Heath Ledger in 2008's *The Dark Knight*.

'The Clown Prince of Crime' was Batman's first truly worthy opponent; more than any other single character, he put supervillains on the map, even starring occasionally in his own comic. Curiously, other than in the 1989 movie, where it was given as 'Jack', he has never been accorded a real name.

Lex Luthor

Having created a hero with such immense power as Superman, Jerry Siegel and Joe Shuster needed to come up with a suitable antagonist. Rather than opting for brute strength, they chose to fight brawn with brain. Lex Luthor arrived in 1940, two years into Superman's run. Referred to as simply 'Luthor' in his debut appearance, the villain evolved into the Man of Steel's most persistent foe. He possessed no superpowers, although he occasionally used science to acquire them. Instead, Luthor was the epitome of the mad scientist, bent on killing Superman as a stepping-stone to world, and universal, domination. He repeatedly escaped from prison to renew his quest to conquer the world.

Initially, Luthor had a full head of red hair but a mistake in the Superman newspaper strip saw him depicted as bald. The new look, later explained as the result of a chemical accident, stuck and became the character's trademark. The same early-Sixties tale revealed that Luthor was a

▶ Lex Luthor, on the edge.

▶▶ Magneto, master strategist.

boyhood friend of Clark Kent, elements familiar to viewers of the *Smallville* television series.

John Byrne's 1986 revamp of Superman recast Lex Luthor in more realistic fashion as a Machiavellian figure, the scheming head of a nefarious multinational corporation. In this incarnation, his ginger hair was shown to be slowly receding. This interpretation has prevailed, although some would prefer to see the return of the classic mad scientist. In 2000, the new Luthor rose as high as President of the United States of America until deposed by the actions of superheroes led by Superman.

Lex Luthor vies with the Joker for the title of DC's greatest supervillain. The theme of science versus superheroics runs through his conflict with the Man of Steel. Luthor's main asset remains brainpower; he cannot outfight Superman, but he can outthink him.

Magneto and Dark Phoenix

It was not until the second coming of the X-Men in the late Seventies that Magneto's potential was fully realised. From the start, his motivation was the protection of mutants from the bigotry of the human race. Underlining the racial conflict metaphor, he was eventually given a background as an Auschwitz survivor. A ruptured friendship with X-Men leader Charles Xavier was woven into his past. Magneto's powers were greatly increased over the years, his control of all kinds of metal eventually making him almost invulnerable. He has been cast as villain, antihero and even, latterly, as a heroic figure. The character's complexities were memorably captured by Sir Ian McKellen in the *X-Men* movies.

The giant robotic Sentinels were introduced in the original run of *X-Men*. Created to capture and nullify mutants, they were brought back early in the renewed series. The plotline involved the X-Men being abducted by the Sentinels and taken to a space station. Returning

to earth in a shuttle, they are saved from destruction by the telekinetic powers of

▶ Magneto, showing his control of all things magnetic.

▶▶ Thanos throws Spider-Man.

Marvel Girl Jean Grey. Apparently killed, Grey is reborn as Phoenix, a being of immense power. Because of interference by the evil Hellfire Club, she is later corrupted into Dark Phoenix and goes on a rampage, destroying an inhabited planet in the process. Editor Jim Shooter forced Chris Claremont and John Byrne to change their original ending where Phoenix survives to one where she pays the ultimate price for her actions, a plotline adopted in *X-Men 3: Last Stand*.

Death is rarely permanent for superheroes and a few years later the original X-Men line-up was reunited when Jean Grey was discovered alive. Her Phoenix incarnation was explained as a manifestation of the cosmic Phoenix Force. Nevertheless, the idea of the dark side of a hero becoming a threat was highly influential in superhero comics and beyond.

Thanos

A virtually all-powerful cosmic supervillain, Thanos made a low-key debut in an issue of *Iron Man* in 1973, going on to become as popular as some of the Marvel heroes who opposed him. The character is often compared to DC's Darkseid in appearance, origins and modus operandi.

Vietnam veteran Jim Starlin was breaking into comics in the early to mid Seventies, initially as a penciller but quickly taking on the writing duties on his first major assignment *Captain Marvel*. The hero, alongside the Avengers, tried to prevent Thanos from acquiring the Cosmic Cube, a device which allows its bearer to shape reality. Thanos became briefly omnipotent but was foiled when Captain Marvel shattered the cube.

The villain's next appearance was in another Starlin series, *Warlock*, where at first he posed as the hero's ally, eventually revealing a mad plan to extinguish every star in the heavens as an offering to Death. This was the key to Thanos' character – his name was derived from a minor Greek personification of death *Thanatos* which Starlin came across in psychology class. He was in love with Mistress Death who appeared variously as a beautiful young woman and a cadaver.

Starlin based much of the character's background on Greek mythology. Thanos was the son of Mentor, leader of a race of gods living on Titan, a moon of Jupiter. Due to a quirk of fate, he evolved into the most powerful of

the Titans, enhancing his already god-like powers with mysticism and bionic technology. He took control of Titan and used it as the launch-pad for his schemes.

Returning to his most famous creation in the early Nineties and since, Starlin has seen Thanos continuing to woo Mistress Death and being foiled by Marvel's superheroes; it generally takes a lot of them to stop him.

▶ Thanos demonstrates his strength.

The Creators

It took men with fertile minds and wild imaginations to create the superheroes we've come to know and love. They were drawn from all walks of life, and while some prospered others were treated harshly by the comics industry. Rarely profiled, this is their story.

Steve Ditko

Notorious for his refusal to be interviewed, photographed or filmed, Steve Ditko was born in Johnstown, Pennsylvania in 1927. He studied under Batman artist Jerry Robinson at the Cartoonists and Illustrators School in New York and began working professionally in comic books in 1953. Ditko co-created the nuclear superhero Captain Atom for Charlton Publications in 1960 during the first of several stints at the company.

Although he was not Stan Lee's first choice as artist on Spider-Man, Ditko contributed a great deal to the character, designing the costume and coming up with the web spray gimmick and his artwork grounded the hero in the real world. In addition to Spider-Man, Ditko devised Marvel's mystical superhero Dr Strange with Lee, where he proved his versatility with some striking 'head trip' art. Ditko also drew the relaunched Hulk series and, briefly, pencilled Iron Man.

He left Spider-Man, and Marvel, after 38 issues, having been latterly credited also as co-plotter. This

▶ Steve Ditko's self portrait.

▶▶ An example of Steve Ditko's work.

followed a disagreement with Lee, reportedly over the identity of the villainous Green Goblin, something which he has denied whilst refusing to elucidate. Returning to Charlton, he worked on their superheroes Blue Beetle, the Question and Captain Atom. This was followed by a short spell at DC where he created the Creeper and the Hawk and the Dove before another interlude at Charlton.

Ditko's 1967 independent creation Mr A reflected his strong moral stance and interest in the objectivist principles of right-wing philosopher Ayn Rand. The late Seventies saw him working for the two major comic-book publishers again. He devised *Shade The Changing Man* for DC, took over from Jack Kirby on *Machine Man* and co-created *Captain Universe*, 'The superhero who could be you!', both for Marvel. His idiosyncratic Missing Man featured as a back-up strip for Pacific Comics in the Eighties. Steve Ditko retired from comics in 1998.

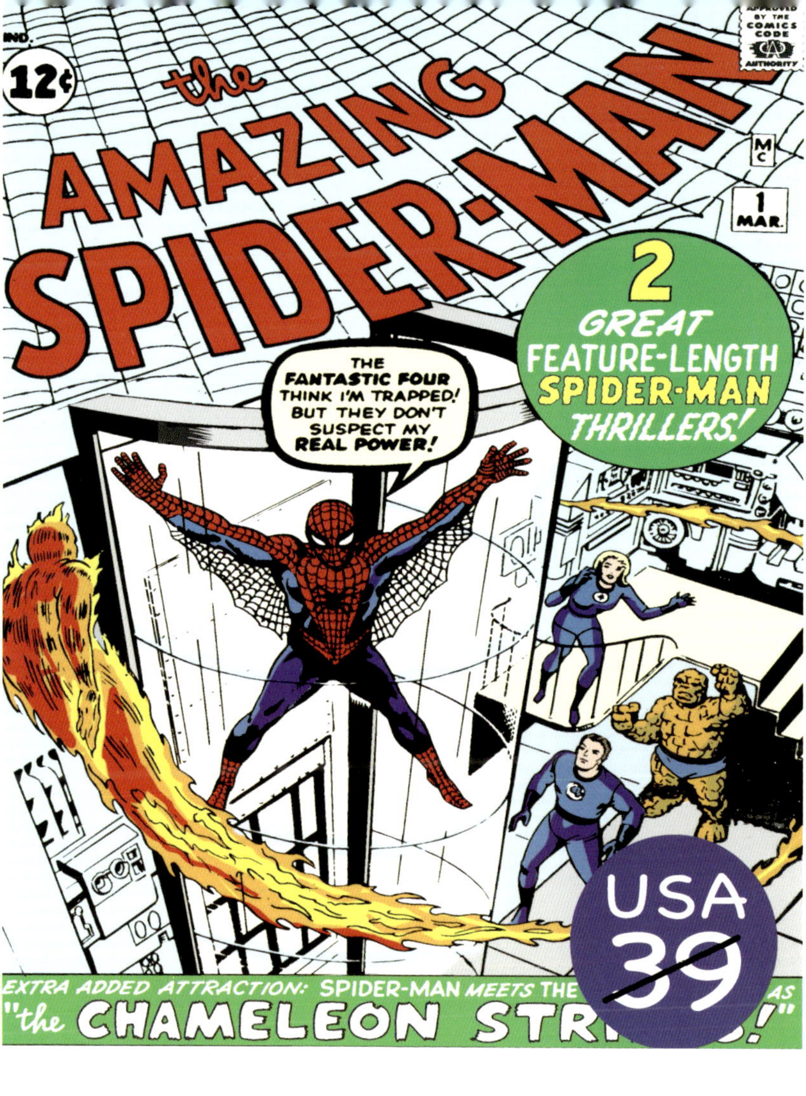
12¢
BY THE COMICS CODE AUTHORITY
the AMAZING SPIDER-MAN
1 MAR.
2 GREAT FEATURE-LENGTH SPIDER-MAN THRILLERS!
THE FANTASTIC FOUR THINK I'M TRAPPED! BUT THEY DON'T SUSPECT MY REAL POWER!
USA 39
EXTRA ADDED ATTRACTION: SPIDER-MAN MEETS THE
"the CHAMELEON STR

Gardner Fox

Born in Brooklyn in 1911, Gardner Fox was inspired by the works of early science-fiction writers, in particular Edgar Rice Burroughs and his *John Carter Of Mars* series. He studied law and was admitted to the New York Bar but, after a couple of years in practice, turned his hand instead to writing comics for DC.

Fox's first superhero creation was the original Sandman. He contributed many early Batman tales, helping Bob Kane and Bill Finger to develop the character, and would return to the Caped Crusader in the Sixties. The Flash was to prove his most popular Golden Age hero, spinning off into appearances in several comics. Debuting at the same time as the Flash was Hawkman, another long-term DC stalwart; Starman and Dr Fate also sprang from his inventive mind.

As head writer for DC's sister company All-American, Fox set the template for the adventures of the Justice Society of America. During the war, he filled in for other writers who had been drafted, working for various companies including Marvel's predecessor Timely.

Turning his hand to other genres whilst superheroes were out of fashion, he was called in by editor Julius Schwartz to help with the revival of DC's costumed adventurers, overseeing the revival of Flash, Hawkman and the Atom and creating the Justice League of America. His *Flash Of Two Worlds* story inaugurated the DC multiverse. Writing Batman again, he revived long-neglected villains Riddler and Scarecrow.

Parting company with DC in 1968 after they refused to grant health benefits to its older creators, he worked briefly for Marvel and wrote numerous novels. He died in 1986.

One of the most prolific comics writers ever, Gardner Fox made an almost incalculable contribution to superhero mythology, creating numerous significant characters and concepts.

Hawkman.

Bob Kane and Bill Finger

Having originated the costumed adventurer – the term 'superhero' had not yet been coined – DC let it be known that they were looking for more such characters. Bob Kane, a fill-in artist on humour strips, was keen to earn more money and took editor Vincent Sullivan up on the suggestion. Generating the idea for Batman over the course of a weekend, he took inspiration from pulp magazine characters like Zorro and the Shadow whose alter ego was a rich socialite. Kane also drew on newspaper strips like *Dick Tracy*, Da Vinci's sketches of a flying machine with bat-like wings and early horror movies *The Bat Whisperers* and 1931's *Dracula* starring Bela Lugosi.

Kane sought help from acquaintance Bill Finger, a pulp writer who was breaking into comics. Finger reworked Kane's original drawings, made suggestions like adding a cowl and a cape instead of batwings and christened the new hero's secret identity Bruce Wayne. Kane credited Finger with making Batman a detective as well as a

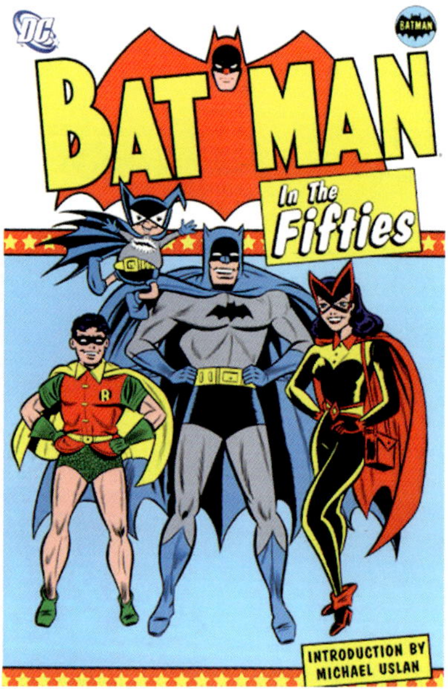

▶ A Batman novel illustrated by Bob Kane.

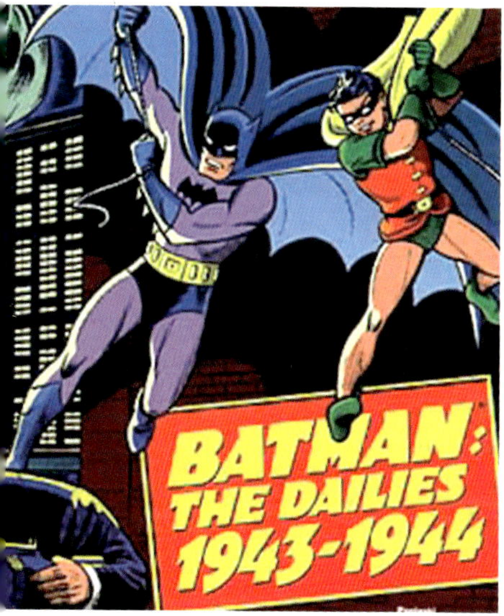

vigilante. The two worked on Batman for many years until Finger's problems with deadlines led to his replacement.

The strip was credited to Kane alone in the days when comic creators were not always acknowledged. It is said that DC were unaware of Finger's input for several issues. Kane's by-line on Batman resulted from a legal agreement with DC which gave him a profit-share in return for surrendering the copyright to the character. Kane, who died in 1998, became a wealthy man; his signature continued to appear on Batman comics for many years, even when the art was ghosted by other hands.

Finger, who contributed much of the mythos and wrote Batman stories for 20 years, received no formal or financial recognition for his contribution to the character. He worked on many other DC characters and died in 1974.

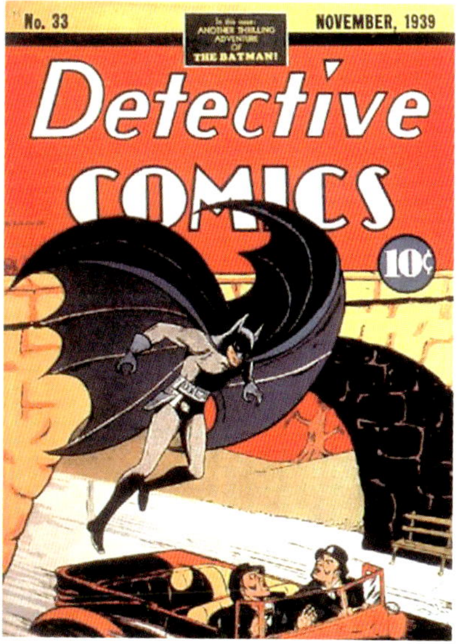

◀ A collection of stories by Bob Kane.

▼ One of the Batman comics that Bob Kane worked on.

Jack Kirby

The ultimate superhero artist, Jack Kirby was one of comics' most prolific creators, producing an astonishing 25,000 pages of artwork in a career which spanned half a century.

Nicknamed 'King' Kirby by Stan Lee, he was born Jacob Kurtzberg in New York in 1917. A self-taught artist, Kirby worked in newspaper strips and animation before teaming up with Joe Simon at Fox Studios in 1939. The pair created the million-selling *Captain America* for Timely in 1940, defecting to DC shortly afterwards. When Kirby returned from the army, the partnership was rekindled but, following the failure of their own company Mainline in 1954, they split up. Kirby went on to work mainly for DC on *Green Arrow* and *Challengers Of The Unknown*. A dispute over a newspaper strip led him to join Atlas (formerly Timely, soon to be Marvel) in 1957.

With Stan Lee, Kirby co-created Fantastic Four, Hulk, Avengers, X-Men and Mighty Thor as well as a host of villains and supporting characters, drawing countless of pages and covers and providing layouts for others to follow. The first artist to use full-page panels, double-page spreads and to choreograph fight scenes, Kirby's style changed during the Sixties; his figures became chunkier,

▶ Jack Kirby produced the artwork for many *Captain America* comics.

▶▶ The second of Jack Kirby's *Fourth World* series.

their anatomy more exaggerated.

Dissatisfied with the lack of credit for writing storylines, Kirby was lured back to DC in 1970 by the promise of artistic control. His *Fourth World* saga was a groundbreaking series of interlinked titles with gods as superheroes. Editorial interference saw him back at Marvel in 1975, where he returned to *Captain America* and devised various new concepts.

In 1978, he left comics to work in animation, taking time out in 1981 to pioneer the direct-sales market with Pacific's *Captain Victory*. His final work was *Superpowers*, a tie-in for a range of toys featuring DC's major superheroes. Jack Kirby died in 1994.

◀ The Forever People from Jack Kirby's *Fourth World*.

Stan Lee

Reserving his given name for his great American novel, Stanley Lieber became Stan Lee for comics work which began with a text page in *Captain America.* Born in New York in 1922, the 18-year-old Lee was originally employed as a gofer in Timely, the comics division of the publishing business owned by relative-by-marriage Martin Goodman. A voracious reader with theatrical leanings, Lee quickly graduated to comic-scripting and was fast-tracked to editor in 1941 when Joe Simon and Jack Kirby left.

Goodman's strategy was to follow prevailing trends and pump out as much product as possible. In 1957, however, a distribution crisis decimated the company's output, leaving a handful of non-superhero titles. In 1961, Goodman instructed Lee, who claimed to be on the verge of quitting comics, to produce a copy of DC's best-selling *Justice League of America.* Lee and artist Jack Kirby came up with *Fantastic Four*, the first of several co-creations which changed the face of superhero comics.

Lee developed a chatty, irreverent style, full of alliteration and asides to the reader, which combined boastfulness with mock-humility and Shakespearean flourishes. His notion of a shared universe in which superheroes regularly interacted was hugely influential and he pioneered full creator credits.

A tireless promoter of Marvel, Stan Lee succeeded Goodman as publisher in 1972 after which his scriptwriting took a back seat. He moved to Los Angeles in 1981 to work on movie and television deals. When Marvel superhero movies took off in the new millennium, Lee made cameo appearances in several. In a surprise return to comics with old rivals DC, he re-imagined many of their leading characters. In 2005, he successfully sued Marvel over the profit share of the

▶ Stan Lee and Jack Kirby co-created *Fantastic Four*.

◀ Stan Lee at an *X-Men* première.

films. Lee remains active in cinema, television and comics, typified by his role in reality TV show *Who Wants To Be A Superhero?*

Frank Miller

Born in Maryland in 1957, Frank Miller came to New York in 1978 with the intention of establishing himself as a comic-book artist. His first published work was for Gold Key on their adaptation of television's *Twilight Zone*. After some fill-in work for Marvel, he successfully lobbied editor Jim Shooter for the job of regular artist on *Daredevil*, beginning in May 1979.

Miller brought a diversity of influences to Marvel's superhero comics which were still largely dominated by the influence of Jack Kirby. As well as hard-boiled crime fiction, Miller was inspired by 1950's EC comics, in particular artist Bernie Krigstein, Japanese manga and film noir. At first drawing then co-plotting the series, he took full creative control of *Daredevil* in January 1981, completing the transformation of a second-string title into Marvel's most talked-about comic.

▶ An early edition of *Daredevil*.

After leaving *Daredevil*, he worked with Chris Claremont on X-Man Wolverine's first solo outing, a four-issue mini series, then moved to DC where he produced the creator-owned *Ronin*. His reputation was sealed by one of the major comics of the Eighties, trailblazing future Batman story *The Dark Knight Returns*; a sequel, *The Dark Knight Strikes Again*, was published in 2001. As writer, he re-imagined the character's origins in *Batman: Year One* in 1987 and returned to *Daredevil* in a similar capacity for a graphic novel, *Love And War* and the *Born Again* storyline in the character's regular title. His 1990 series *Elektra Lives Again*, drawn in experimental style, resurrected Daredevil's erstwhile lover, whilst in 1993, he revamped the hero's origin again in the mini-series *The Man Without Fear*.

◀ Frank Miller directed *The Spirit*.

In the early Nineties he wrote the screenplays for *Robocop* 2 and 3. Miller went on to co-direct the movie adaptation of his hard-boiled comics series *Sin City* in 2005 and directed the 2008 film version of Will Eisner's superhero *The Spirit*.

Alan Moore

Alan Moore was born in Northampton in 1953. Expelled from school at 17 for dealing in LSD, he worked as a toilet cleaner in an abattoir before deciding to make use of the creative skills he learnt at Northampton Arts Lab. Moore specifically targeted comics as a medium where he could make an impact as a writer.

Starting with fillers for *Doctor Who* magazine and *2000 AD*, his first two regular series were *V For Vendetta* and *Marvelman* in British independent monthly *Warrior*. *Marvelman*, a startling revival of a long-defunct character, was the first of Moore's deconstructed superheroes. His version of *Captain Britain* for Marvel UK, which appeared simultaneously, was more conventional but no less imaginative.

Moore's growing reputation saw him headhunted by DC. His first series for the company was *Swamp Thing*, a horror comic which established his reputation stateside. After fill-ins on Superman, Batman and other DC heroes, he co-created *Watchmen* with British artist Dave Gibbons. This further deconstructed the superhero myth and is now regarded as a classic.

Marvelman became *Miracleman* for the American market and the much-delayed saga reached a visceral conclusion in 1988. After falling into dispute with DC, Moore left mainstream comics to set up his own short-lived imprint Mad Love, the failure of which led him to work with the Image creators on their superheroes and on his own early Marvel parody/homage *1963*.

Image founder Jim Lee offered

▶ Alan Moore.

◀ A pyrotechnics display at the première of the film *V For Vendetta*.

Moore his own imprint under the WildStorm banner. America's Best Comics began with *The League of Extraordinary Gentlemen*, a teaming of Victorian heroes and continued with 'science hero' *Tom Strong*, Gnostic superheroine *Promethea* and *Top 10*, a series about policing a city of superpowered inhabitants.

Frequently hailed as the greatest comics scriptwriter of all time, Moore's rigorously intelligent approach has played a major role in the mainstream acceptance of the superhero.

Jerry Siegel and Joe Shuster

Writer Jerry Siegel and artist Joe Shuster (both born in 1914) were shy, bespectacled high-school friends in Cleveland, Ohio sharing a love of science fiction and comic strips. Siegel founded one of the first sci-fi fanzines to which Shuster contributed. In 1935, they broke into comic books, Doctor Occult appearing in DC's *More Fun* whilst Slam Bradley featured in early issues of *Detective Comics*.

Their original Super-Man was a villain from a short story in a fanzine. Siegel came up with the revised concept in 1934 during a sleepless night. For five years, the pair tried to sell Superman as a newspaper strip. Sheldon Mayer, assistant editor at the McClure syndicate, saw some potential but was unable to persuade his boss, Max Gaines, to take it up. Gaines felt the idea was unsuitable for newspapers but might work in comics and passed it on to Vincent Sullivan, a DC editor who was preparing a new title, *Action Comics*. Sullivan persuaded publisher

▶ Superman first appeared in *Action Comics*.

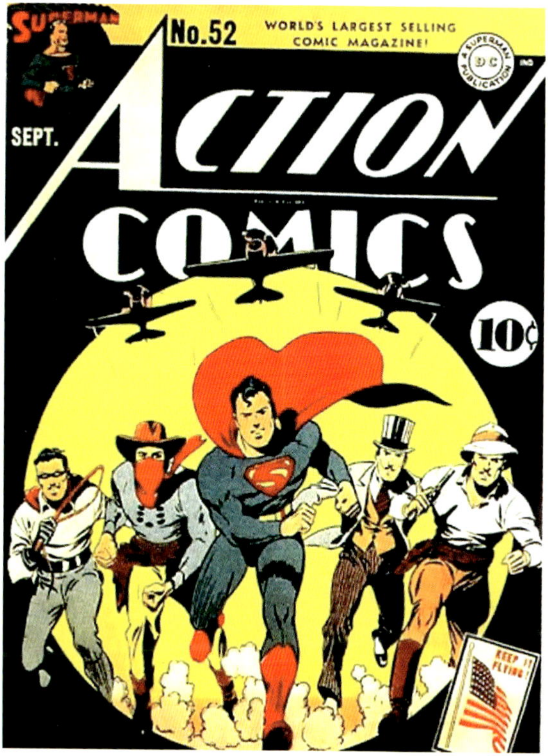

◀ Superman on the cover of *Action Comics*.

Harry Donenfeld to take a chance on Superman and Siegel and Shuster had to quickly rework it from a newspaper strip into a 13-page comic-book story.

Siegel and Shuster sold the rights to the character along with the first story for $130. Their creation soon became not only comics' signature character but a twentieth-century icon. After leaving DC, the pair split up. Whilst Siegel continued writing comics including a stint on British strip *The Spider*, Shuster was eventually forced to give up drawing because of poor eyesight.

Led by Siegel, their legal challenges to DC's ownership of Superman failed but in 1975, after much publicity and concerted pressure from comic-book professionals, the company granted Siegel and Shuster an annual $20,000 pension and creator credits on all Superman material. Shuster died in 1992 and Siegel in 1996.

Superheroes on Screen

From the earliest days of the superhero, radio and film serials helped familiarise the non-comic book-reading public with the characters. Now movies and television allow superheroes to break out of cult status into popular consciousness.

Superman was the first to be adapted for other media when, in 1941, a radio serial helped turn the character into a household name. Running three times a week, the show launched the catchphrase "Up, up and away" and introduced teenage reporter Jimmy Olsen. Kryptonite made its first appearance on the series, while Batman and Robin were regular guests.

In the era before television, 12 or 15-part weekly movie serials were massively popular. When negotiations in 1941 broke down over the rights to use Superman, Republic Pictures turned to Fawcett Publications, producing the *Adventures of Captain Marvel* instead. Columbia made Batman the first DC character to make the transition to live action in the cheaply-made 1943 serial which added Bruce Wayne's butler Alfred to the character's world. A sequel, *Batman And Robin*, appeared five years later.

Timely's major superhero Captain America was given the Hollywood treatment by Republic in 1944. Apart from the name and costume, little survived of the comic-book character as the screen

version carried a gun, had a female sidekick and was an attorney in his secret identity.

Superman featured in a series of groundbreaking animated features produced by the Fleischer/Famous Studio between 1941 and 1943 but had to wait until 1948 for his big screen debut when he was played by Kirk Alyn. The eponymous Columbia serial spawned a 1950 sequel, *Atom Man Vs Superman* featuring a villain created for the radio show, which ended in 1951. The same year an hour-long movie *Superman And The Mole Men* was produced. Effectively a pilot for

▼ The outfit worn by Christopher Reeve in the *Superman* movies.

the television show *The Adventures Of Superman*, it featured the man who made the title role his own, George Reeves. The show ran for six seasons from 1951 to 1958, the final three filmed in colour.

Cartoons starring superheroes were a staple of American TV's Saturday-morning kids' programming but the next live-action superhero made an indelible mark on pop culture. Produced by William Dozier for the ABC network, *Batman* had something for all the family – it served up comic-book action for the kids, whilst the adults could appreciate its camp overtones and the deadly serious acting of the principals led by Adam West in the title role and Burt Ward as Robin. Debuting in 1966 and running for three seasons, the show spawned a spin-off movie in its first year. The show's success inspired ABC to revive the masked hero of movie serial hero *Green Hornet*, which featured a young Bruce Lee as sidekick Kato. Lacking Batman's camp appeal, the series was not a hit.

DC's monopoly on small-screen superheroes continued with *Wonder Woman*. There had been an abortive attempt to adapt the character for

◀ Superman holds things together.

television in the Sixties and, in 1974, a TV movie starring Cathy Lee Crosby as a blonde Wonder Woman without superpowers, was aired. ABC produced a more faithful adaptation set during the Second World War, with former Miss USA Lynda Carter perfectly filling the figure-hugging costume. After one season, an almost unprecedented change of network to CBS saw the setting updated – this remains without explanation to the present day.

Marvel finally got in on the act in 1978 when *The Incredible Hulk* became the first of the company's superheroes to successfully graduate to live action. The show starred Bill Bixby as David Banner – bizarrely, 'Bruce' was deemed 'too gay' – and bodybuilder Lou Ferrigno as the creature. A ratings-topper on both sides of the Atlantic, *The Incredible Hulk* owed a great deal of its success to the fact that it bore little resemblance to the comic, favouring human-interest stories rather than the comic's monosyllabic, angry Hulk battling supervillains. Though the series was cancelled in 1982, three television movie sequels were made in the late Eighties; the first two, *The Incredible Hulk Returns* and *The Trail of the Incredible Hulk*, were effectively

◀ Tobey Maguire poses in front of a poster for *Spider-Man* 3 .

unsuccessful back-door pilots for prospective *Thor* and *Daredevil* series. The Hulk was apparently killed in the final film, appropriately entitled *The Death Of The Incredible Hulk.*

Spider-Man fared less well. Some 15 episodes of a television series starring Nicholas Hammond as the wall-crawler were aired between 1977 and 1979 but the special effects were unconvincing and even Stan Lee, credited as a script consultant, was moved to criticise it as 'too juvenile'. The trilogy of movies, beginning with 2002's *Spider-Man*, suffered no such shortcomings pleasing fans and critics alike and performing well at the box-office.

Star Wars paved the way for futuristic fantasy to return to cinemas and in 1978 the first big-budget superhero blockbuster hit the screens. *Superman The Movie*, starring Christopher Reeve, retained much of the mythology of the original comics and, for the first time, special-effects technology was able to deliver the tagline "You'll believe a man can fly." The three sequels – *Superman II*, *III* and *IV: The Quest For Peace* – were less successful and the franchise went into hibernation for almost 20 years. The Man of Steel's cousin,

▶ Lynda Carter as Wonder Woman.

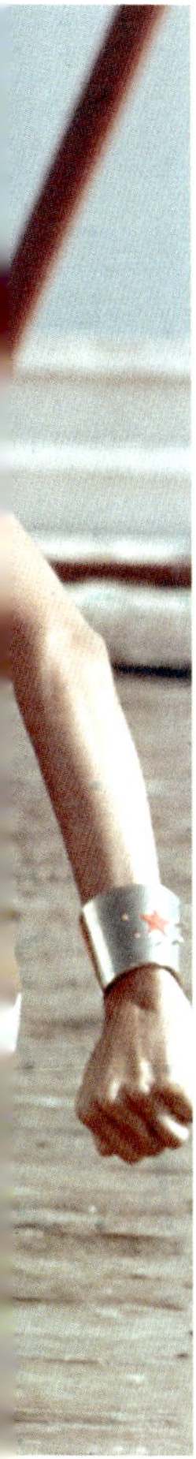

Supergirl, was the subject of a 1984 effort starring Helen Slater in the title role and featuring legendary English comedian Peter Cook in a rare Hollywood excursion.

Whilst absent from the cinemas, Superman lived again on television with the largely faithful adaptation *Lois And Clark: The New Adventures Of Superman* (1993-1997) featuring Dean Cain as Superman/Clark Kent and Terri Hatcher as Lois Lane. Clark Kent's pre-Superman boyhood and origins were the subject of the long-running *Smallville* (2001 onwards). Superman was reintroduced to cinema-goers in 2006's lacklustre *Superman Returns*, directed by Bryan Singer who helmed the first two *X-Men* pictures.

Re-runs of the Sixties *Batman* television series were still commonplace in 1989 when a darker interpretation of the hero's world was presented. The Oscar-winning *Batman* starred Michael Keaton in the title role and Jack Nicholson as a convincingly crazy Joker. This also spawned three sequels, with Val Kilmer and George Clooney successively succeeding Keaton as Wayne/Batman in the final two. 1997's *Batman And Robin* proved unpopular with audiences and critics and the franchise went on hold for eight years until rebooted in *Batman Begins*. Christian Bale took the title role which he reprised in 2008 in *The Dark Knight* featuring the late Heath Ledger as the Joker, the actor's penultimate movie role.

Following the box-office success of *Batman*, Sam Raimi created a superhero specifically for the cinema. *Darkman* (1990) starred Liam Neeson and went on to generate two direct-to-video sequels. Also, reversing the usual order of things, the character of Darkman went from movies to appearing in comics. Other original cinematic superheroes include Disney's *Sky High* (2005), the critically panned *Zoom* (2006) and Will Smith's comedy drama *Hancock* (2008).

Marvel superheroes enjoyed a less impressive profile on the big screen featuring in low-budget versions of *The Punisher* (1989) and *Captain America*

▶ A promotional poster for *X-Men Origins: Wolverine*.

(1990), an unreleased adaptation of *Fantastic Four* (1994) and the unpopular *Howard The Duck* (1986). The first Marvel character to make an impact in movies was a minor character from their Seventies Dracula series, the vampire killer *Blade* in 1998.

The new millennium saw the superhero movie come of age, and most of Marvel's major characters have transferred to the cinema. X-Men led the way with a trilogy of movies followed by an Origins series, starting with Wolverine in 2009. *Spider-Man*, *Fantastic Four*, *Iron Man*, *The Punisher*, *Daredevil* and *Elektra* followed. *The Hulk* was successfully rebooted by French director Louis Leterrier in 2008 after the Ang Lee-directed 2003 adaptation failed.

The appetite for superhero films continued unquenched throughout the decade. DC's *Watchmen*, partly an exercise in exploiting the unique grammar of comics and deemed 'unfilmable' by co-creator Alan Moore, made it into cinemas in 2009 after many years in development hell.

Superheroes can be played for laughs as in the BBC sitcom *My Hero* or ITV2's *No Heroics*, and the genre

▶ Tim Kring.

is ripe for parody, as demonstrated by the 2008's *Superhero Movie*. Meanwhile Tim Kring's *Heroes* television series (2007 onwards) took on board many of the traditional elements of the superhero, yet avoided referring to its protagonists as such. Knowingly borrowing comics' story-arc structure and paying explicit homage to its sources with various references and in-jokes, *Heroes* showed how superheroes could be portrayed without costumes and secret identities.

Boasting a winning combination of exaggerated action, fantasy and timeless good-versus-evil conflict, superheroes on screen rank as potential blockbusters and look set to be around for a long time to come.

Quotes and Catchphrases

Every superhero needs a catchphrase – here are some of the most famous, plus some words of wisdom from their creators.

◀ The Hulk in action.

"Criminals are a superstitious cowardly lot." Bruce 'Batman' Wayne

"With great power there must also come great responsibility." Caption in the first Spider-Man story

"Hulk will smash!" "Hulk is the strongest of them all." The Incredible Hulk

"Your friendly neighbourhood Spider-Man." The Amazing Spider-Man

"Don't make me angry, you wouldn't like me when I'm angry." David Banner, alter ego of TV's Incredible Hulk

"In brightest day, in darkest night, no evil will escape my sight. Let those who worship evil's might, beware my power! Green Lantern's light." Green Lantern's oath

"Anger? By the bristling beard of Odin thou knowest not the meaning of the word!" The Mighty Thor

"He's cheated death so often, you just can't trust that guy." Robin on the Joker

"Some girls love to have a man stronger than they are to make them do things. Do I like it? I don't know, it's sort of thrilling. But isn't it more fun to make a man obey?" Wonder Woman

"I'm the best there is at what I do. But what I do best isn't very nice." Wolverine

"Faster than a speeding bullet! More powerful than a locomotive! Able to leap tall buildings with a single bound! Look! Up in the sky! It's a bird! It's a plane! It's Superman!" Introduction to the *Superman* radio series

"Tune in next week, same bat-time, same bat-channel." Closing voiceover, *Batman* TV show

"Jerry reversed the usual formula of the superhero who goes to another planet. He put the superhero in ordinary, familiar surroundings instead of the other way around, as was done in most science fiction. That was the first time I can recall that it had ever been done." Joe Shuster

"Vengeance is a great reason. It would take all the violence, the rage he felt inside over his parents' murder to fight injustice. It motivated him to take his revenge on all the criminal element." Bob Kane on Batman

"When I do a job, it's not my personality that I'm offering the readers but my artwork. It's not what I'm like

that counts; it's what I did and how well it was done... I produce a product, a comic art story. Steve Ditko is the brand name."
Steve Ditko

"We'll do a superhero team, but let's make it different."
Stan Lee on creating Fantastic Four

"Stan Lee and I never collaborated on anything! I've never seen Stan Lee write anything! I used to write all the stories just like I always did!"
Jack Kirby in 1988

"I've always felt guilty about what happened to comics after *Watchmen*. I really did open the floodgates on a lot of pretension..."
Alan Moore

◀ Thor displaying his anger.

▼ Batman and Robin weigh up the situation.

"The fundament of a superhero is the guy in tights saving innocent people from bad things. It's amazing how infrequently that seems to happen in superhero comics these days."
Frank Miller

"There are men so godlike, so exceptional, that they naturally, by right of their extraordinary gifts, transcend all moral judgment or constitutional control. There is no law which embraces men of that calibre. They are themselves law."
Aristotle

Superhero Trivia

Think you know all there is to know about superheroes? We have some wild facts to make you think again!

- The first issue of *Whiz Comics* was actually number 2. Number 1 was an 'ashcan' edition, a dummy used to secure copyright on the title.
- Stan Lee wanted to call X-Men the Mutants but publisher Martin Goodman disagreed, believing that the readership would not understand the word.
- Wonder Woman was originally to be called 'Suprema the Wonder Woman'.
- The Hulk was originally coloured grey but early-Sixties printing technology could not produce a consistent shade. One test example came out green, which Stan Lee preferred.
- Spider-Man actor Tobey Maguire has never read any of the comics featuring the character.
- Superman first flew in animated cartoons, as it was easier to show him flying than to have him crouch and leap.
- Seventies rock band The Teardrop Explodes took their name from a caption in a *Daredevil* comic.

▼ *Whiz Comics* had no number 1 issue.

▶ A grey Hulk.

- The next-issue box at the end of Thor's first appearance misspells the hero's name as 'Thorr'.

- The final two issues of Captain America's original comic were entitled *Captain America's Terror Tales* and did not feature the character or any superheroes.

- Actor Cesar Romero refused to shave off his moustache when playing the Joker in the *Batman* TV series, so his white face make-up was applied over it.

- In 1966, Pittsburgh Steelers American Football team adopted a new uniform, the design of which was influenced by the Batman outfits from the television show.

- In 2008, the Joker was voted the greatest supervillain of all-time in a survey conducted in Manchester's Arndale Centre.

- Jack Kirby made a cameo appearance in an episode of *The Incredible Hulk* TV show.

- The two-word version of 'super hero' is registered as a trademark in America and is jointly owned by Marvel and DC.

- Predating the Fantastic Four by six months, the short-lived Dr Droom (later renamed Dr Druid) was actually Marvel's first Silver Age superhero.

- Christopher Walken, Jon Voight, Nick Nolte, Arnold Schwarzenegger and

Neil Diamond were considered for the title part in *Superman The Movie*, before the producers cast Christopher Reeve.

- Early superhero comics were not officially distributed in Britain but were brought over as ship's ballast and then sold off.
- The first female superhero was Fantomah who appeared in *Jungle Comics*, published by Fiction House in 1940.
- The first gay superhero was Northstar, a member of Marvel's Canadian Alpha Flight team; his sexuality was revealed in 1992.

◀ Northstar, the first gay superhero.

- Marvel's Black Panther who debuted in 1966, was the first non-stereotyped black superhero.
- As well as cartoons, television and films, Superman was the subject of an off-Broadway musical comedy in 1966.
- Marvel claimed their late-Seventies character the Human Fly was "The wildest superhero ever because he's real!" It was based on stuntman Rick Rojatt.
- In 2003, members of the pressure group Fathers 4 Justice staged a protest at Buckingham Palace dressed as Batman and Robin with a banner reading 'Super Dads of Fathers 4 Justice'.
- The first British superhero was the Amazing Mr X who appeared in *The Dandy* in August 1944.
- Superman's first UK appearance was in the weekly paper *Triumph* in August 1939.

▶ Shuri, the new Black Panther.

Superhero Collectables

Hold onto your wallets as we present a guide to the top 10 most collectable comics of all time!

10. WHIZ COMICS 1

(Fawcett, February 1940)

Fawcett Publication's first comic book was originally dubbed *Flash Comics*, but DC had claimed that name so it was changed to *Thrill Comics*. However, another company had come up with *Thrilling Comics* and Fawcett finally settled on *Whiz Comics*. Lead character Captain Marvel made his first appearance here. The cover was remarkably similar to *Action Comics* 1, the superhero demonstrating his strength by manhandling a car, something which may well have alerted DC whose lawyers soon instigated the long-running battle over the alleged plagiarism of Superman.

Near Mint Value: £39,000-£41,000

9. MORE FUN COMICS 52

(DC, February 1940)

Superman co-creator Jerry Siegel also came up with the Spectre, a mystical superhero drawn by Bernard Baily. Murdered cop Jim Corrigan is brought back to life by a mysterious disembodied presence to fight crime as the ghostly Spectre, a being of seemingly infinite power. In *More Fun Comics* 52 the Spectre's official debut is limited to a single panel at the end of the story. The original series lasted until 1945 although the character has been revived several times since. Curiously, the Spectre's name has always been spelt in the British way rather than Specter.

Near Mint Value: £41,000-£43,000

▶ An example of an early *All-American* comic.

8. FLASH COMICS 1

(All-American, January 1940)

DC's sister company, All-American, was headed by Maxwell Gaines, one of the pioneers of the American comic-book format. Several of DC's enduring heroes including Wonder Woman and Green Lantern actually originated under the All-American banner. *Flash Comics* 1 represented its first foray into superhero territory with the Golden Age debuts of the Flash and Hawkman. The title also featured Johnny Thunder, the Whip and Cliff Cornwall but it was the two superheroes who remained the star attractions of *Flash Comics*.

Near Mint Value: £54,000-£56,000

7. CAPTAIN AMERICA COMICS 1

(Timely, March 1941)

Captain America was the first superhero to debut in the first issue in his own title, a measure of the confidence which Timely had in the character. On sale a year before the United States joined the Second World War, the cover depicts Captain America socking Hitler on the jaw, perhaps reflecting the feelings of Jewish co-creators Joe Simon and Jack Kirby. Like many Golden Age comics which sold in huge quantities few copies survive today, partly because Americans were encouraged to recycle comics and magazines to help the war effort.

Near Mint Value: £63,000-£65,000

6. BATMAN 1

(DC, Spring 1940)

The first issue of Batman's own title would be collectable enough in its own right. That it contains the debuts of two legendary supervillains adds to its value and importance, as does the fact that it features Batman's final solo adventures before the arrival of Robin. The Joker crops up in two stories, whilst another introduces the Cat who would soon evolve into Catwoman. Not only that but Batman carried a gun for the last time as DC began adopting a form of self-censorship, eager to present its output as wholesome family entertainment.

Near Mint Value: £66,500-£68,500

5. ALL-AMERICAN COMICS 16

(All-American, July 1940)

The eponymous *All-American Comics* was the first publication by DC's offshoot which came about when owners Jack Liebowitz and Harry Donenfeld disagreed over whether the company's line should expand. This resulted in

Liebowitz going into partnership with Max Gaines for the new imprint. The two companies were linked but separate, each having separate offices and editorial staff. In 1940 All-American publications started to carry the DC logo and the two merged in 1945. *All-American Comics* 16 is prized for the first appearance of the Golden Age Green Lantern.
Near Mint Value: £95,000-£100,000

4. SUPERMAN 1
(DC, Summer 1939)

American comic books were originally 64-page anthology titles. *Superman* 1 was the first title devoted to a single character, a one-off experiment filled by reprints from *Action Comics*. Sufficiently popular to merit an ongoing title featuring new material, it paved the way for the soon-to-be common practice of superheroes starring in their own comics. There was a little 'new' material in *Superman* 1; four pages which had been cut from the character's origin story in *Action Comics* 1 were restored and feature here.
Near Mint Value: £150,000-£160,000

3. MARVEL COMICS 1
(Timely, November 1939)

Pulp publisher Martin Goodman allowed himself to be persuaded by Frank Torpey, sales manager of comic-book production and packaging company Funnies Inc, that there was money in the new medium. The result of the venture was *Marvel Comics*, christened after Goodman's pulp magazine *Marvel Science Stories*. The first issue starred the Human Torch and the Sub-Mariner, whilst supporting features included costumed crime fighter the Angel, Tarzan-like jungle hero Ka-Zar and a Western series, the Masked Raider. For no apparent reason, the title became *Marvel Mystery Comics* with the second issue.
Near Mint Value: £165,000-£175,000

2. DETECTIVE COMICS 27
(DC, May 1939)

Batman, DC's second most popular superhero made his first appearance in the already-existing title *Detective Comics* (from which DC would take its initials). This had previously featured a variety of crime stories, including the exploits of Sax Rohmer's prototype supervillain Fu Manchu. Unusually for a Golden Age superhero debut, the story does not relate Batman's origin, giving the

◀ Part of the very first *Superman* comic.

▶ A *Detective Comics* edition featuring Batman.

▶▶ The cover of the first *Batman* comic.

character added allure and mystery. *Detective Comics* 27 is probably rarer than *Action Comics* 1 because print runs on first issues were traditionally higher.
Near Mint Value:
£190,000-£200,000

1. ACTION COMICS 1

(DC, June 1938)

This is where it all began. The most valuable and significant comic book of all time invented the superhero and gave comics a new direction and impetus the medium had previously lacked. The dramatic, iconic cover promised something very different inside. Superman filled only 13 pages, the other features in *Action* 1 being a motley assortment of long-forgotten boxers, Westerns, ace reporters and historical features plus a cartoon strip. Standard comic-book fare of the era, soon to be swept away by the cult of the superhero.
Near Mint Value:
£275,000-£285,000

Other books also available:

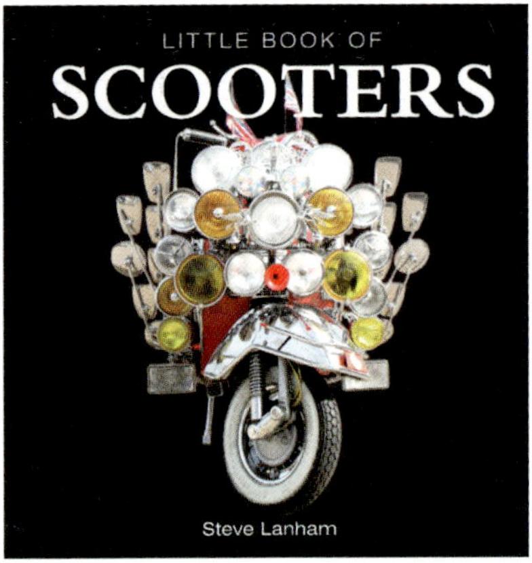

Other books also available:

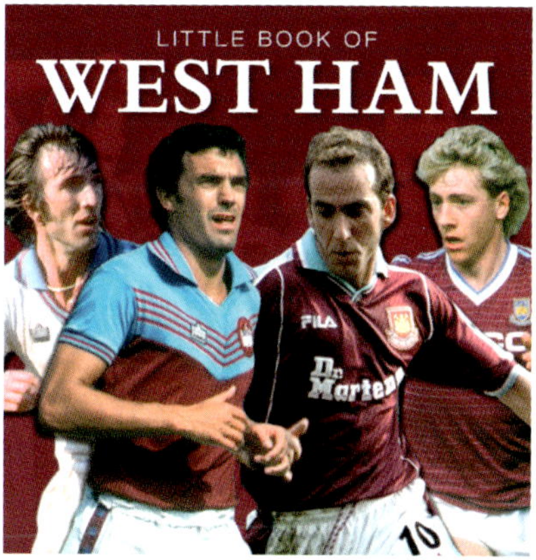

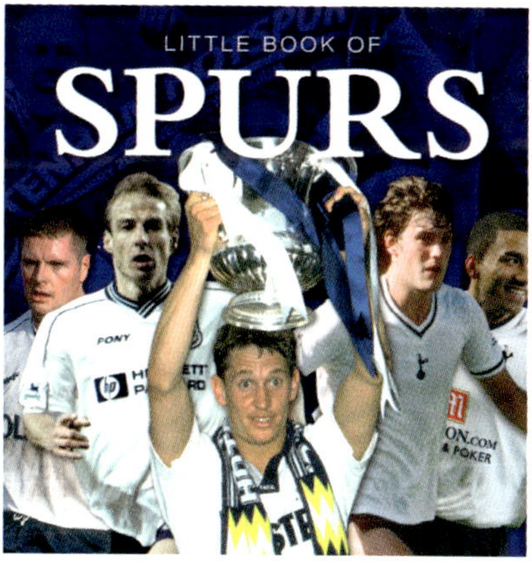

The pictures in this book were provided courtesy of the following:

GETTY IMAGES
101 Bayham Street, London NW1 0AG

Design and Artwork by Scott Giarnese and Jane Stephens

Published by G2 Entertainment Limited

Publishers Jules Gammond and Edward Adams

Written by Mike Gent and Michael Heatley